_____ *Healing and Ev*

Russ Parker was born in Birkenhea[...]
Christian in 1966, has exercised a w[...]
denominations, including the Church[...]
an ordained minister. He has been a c[...]
selling at St John's College, Nottin[...]
several books, including *The Occult: Deliverance from Evil*
(IVP 1989), *Free to Fail* (Triangle 1992), *Healing Dreams* (Triangle 1993) and *Forgiveness is Healing* (Daybreak 1993). Married to Carole, they have two children at university.

Roy Lawrence was born in Eccles, Lancashire. Since his ordination he has served in four northern parishes. Married to Eira, with two grown up sons, he is currently vicar of Prenton, Birkenhead and is also an honorary canon of Chester Cathedral and adviser to the bishop and diocese of Chester in the ministry of healing, as well as being an honorary staff member of the Acord Christian Healing Trust. His previous publications include *Good News about God*: a confirmation course (Countyvise 1988) and *How to Pray When Life Hurts* (IVP USA 1992/SU 1993).

Healing and Evangelism

RUSS PARKER
and ROY LAWRENCE

Roy Lawrence

△
TRIANGLE

First published in Great Britain in 1996

Triangle
SPCK
Holy Trinity Church
Marylebone Road
London NW1 4DU

Biblical quotations are taken from *The New English Bible*
© 1961, 1970 Oxford and Cambridge University Presses and
from *The Revised English Bible* © 1989 Oxford and
Cambridge University Presses.

British Library Cataloguing-in-Publication Data
A catalogue record of this book is available from
the British Library

ISBN 0–281–04777–4

Typeset by Dorwyn Ltd, Rowlands Castle
Printed in Great Britain by BPC Paperbacks Ltd

This book is dedicated to the
members, friends, supporters and staff
of the Acorn Christian Healing Trust
who yearn with us for the conversion and
healing of our nation.

Contents

1 Rediscovering the Evangelizing Church

Not long ago, while conducting a series of meetings in Japan, I was invited to take part in a mission being conducted by an Anglican church in Tonderbaiashi some thirty miles from Osaka. The town is dominated by a 200-foot white tower where prayers are continually offered in memory of those who died in all wars, and which is part of a flourishing local cult. Before the meeting I was sitting in the minister's house which was attached to the church. The vicar, Dennis, came and told me that he had a confession to make. He felt that to some degree he had invited me over to his church under false pretences. In fact there was only one member in his congregation apart from himself, his wife and family and the occasional visitor. Consequently he was not sure if anyone would be attending the service. I asked him how long he had been working in this town and he replied, 'Twelve years'. He had conducted services faithfully throughout those years but had found it very difficult indeed. He felt a failure. I asked why he had stayed so long and he said he believed that someone should live among those people and let them know that God loves them. Needless to say, I was humbled and impressed at his conviction and perseverence: I would have given up long ago!

However, since my partner and I were coming to his country Dennis felt that the church should step out in mission. So he had been around the town to alert people about this meeting in particular. Imagine our surprise when we entered the church to find over twenty people present. It was a lovely opportunity to share something of the love of Jesus Christ and eight people made a commitment of faith as a result. None of them had attended a church before, and I am quite sure that God was rewarding Dennis's faithfulness and prayerfulness for the people he had stepped out to love.

My visit to this church near Osaka reminded me that all over the world God is stirring his church to recover its mission. No longer is this the prerogative of evangelical churches, mission societies or large, well attended churches; it is now happening in churches of every description. Another interesting factor in this current wave of modern evangelization is that it is seriously ecumenical. Eric Delve, one of Britain's most experienced evangelists and now an incumbent in Liverpool, teamed up with Father Pat Lynch, Director of the Sion Catholic Community to conduct evangelistic missions. These were particularly successful and spoke to both Roman Catholic and Anglican communities that the Gospel of Jesus Christ was a shared charge and blessing. In a similar venture of faith and co-operation, one of the missioners for the visit of the evangelist J John to the city of Leeds was the Benedictine monk Father Ian Petit.

Alongside these two initiatives is the example of witness to the city by David Sheppard, the Anglican Bishop of Liverpool and the late Derek Warlock, the Roman Catholic Archbishop of Liverpool. Their book, *With Hope in our Hearts*, charts their united efforts to champion the needs and the talents of the people of Merseyside. They addressed unemployment, poor housing and the need for healing and understanding between the religious communities of that great city. Both David Sheppard and Derek Warlock considered all these activities to be evangelistic and lying at the heart of mission. It is little wonder that all these events are taking place during the Church of

England's Decade of Evangelism and the Roman Catholic Church's Decade for Evangelization.

However, there are more reasons than the decade initiatives to account for the growing involvement in evangelism at parish level. This chapter seeks to answer two basic questions: Why is there a resurgence of mission? and What does this mission consist of? In a later chapter we shall discuss some of the opportunities which seem ready-made for mission within the community and make some suggestions as to how to use these as drawbridges of care and witness into our towns and cities.

Why is there a resurgence of mission?

THE MODEL OF JESUS

Jesus was, and is and will always be the man for others. He is the supreme example of love going out of its way to attend to the needs of others. He announced himself as the one who had been sent and consequently he is the first apostle of mission in the New Testament. In his home town he fittingly described his mission in the synagogue by taking the words of Isaiah 61:

> The Spirit of the Lord is upon me,
> because he has annointed me;
> he has sent me . . . to announce good news to the poor,
> to proclaim release for prisoners
> and recovery of sight for the blind;
> to let the broken victims go free,
> to proclaim the year of the Lord's favour.
>
> Luke 4.18–19 (Revised English Bible)

It is important to see that the model of Jesus's mission is both proactive and reactive according to this declaration of intent. It is proactive in announcing the Good

News which calls people into relationship with God the father through Jesus the son. This also serves as the challenge of mission as it calls us to acknowledge the need for a changed life – a life that is to be lived out according to God's pattern rather than by our own changing values, caprice and prejudices. However, Jesus's care of souls is also reactive in that he seeks to bring the healing and saving love of God to our needs which are often the result of our wrong choices or the result of damage inflicted by others.

These two aspects of mission need to be kept in balance and harmony otherwise we fall into the danger of a gospel of extremes. At one extreme there is the pietistic model, offering a form of salvation which seems to be an escape from the real world into what Os Guiness called the 'Indian reservation of total separation'. It is a privatized fellowship of the elite who have disowned the world as it is. Consequently the focus of its evangelism is on rescuing people from the world rather than bringing restoration to the community.

At the other extreme there is the gospel which is need-centred rather than Christ-centred. The Bishop of the Rio Grand has said that the Church was not brought into being by God to meet the real or felt needs of people. This gospel says, 'You have a need and Jesus can meet it'.[1] Lawrence Crabb identifies a similar trend in the relatively recent emergence of Christian counselling centres in the United States. He writes that the approach to such counselling is to feel better rather than find God.[2] He goes on to say that our primary purpose in counselling is not to use God to solve our problems but to move through our problems towards finding God.[3]

Perhaps midway between these two poles, and yet an extreme gospel in itself, is the one which identifies itself with issues of justice and peace. This has usually been combined with a liberation theology which sees Jesus as not so much a redeemer as a revolutionary who has come to overturn the status quo of the rich in favour of a political equality for all. This emphasis certainly challenges the evangelical to be more concerned about saving the whole person, including their environment and community, rather than just some spiritual package locked up within. I well remember my father saying that during his war experiences in the North African desert and in Germany, the only religious people he could tolerate were the Salvation Army because they really cared about him as a person and not just his soul! He would tell me stories of Salvationists bringing him tea and cigarettes whilst under fire and stopping for a chat when there was time. 'They were like us and shared the same dangers', he said.

It is exciting, then, to see a proliferation of organizations across the country which provide medical and pastoral care in such fields as AIDS counselling and helping the homeless, but at the same time, and in appropriate ways, share something of the saving love of Christ. I am thinking in particular of more recent enterprises such as OASIS which seeks to look after the needs of homeless young people. Then there are the APOSTOLATE projects of the Acorn Christian Healing Trust which combine medical and pastoral skills in a range of concerns from the Losely Christian Cancer Centre near Guildford to the King's House in Gateshead, where troubled people come to receive a ministry of listening and prayer from members of the local churches.

In his mission Jesus perfectly combined the twin elements of challenge and care. He is the love that went out of its way to become incarnate in human flesh and so share from the inside the wounds of living in a fallen world; he is the love that goes out of its way to call strangers to become friends by following him as Lord; he went out of his way to return to a hostile Bethany in

order to raise his friend Lazarus from the dead and restore joy to a grief-stricken family; he went out of his
way when he allowed himself to be publicly compromised by a repentant prostitute looking for forgiveness;
he went out of his way to give time to an outcast
Samaritan woman so that she might find peace of heart.
Love went out of its way ultimately to Calvary and a
cross where all our sins were forgiven and where we now
find release and restoration.

Jesus summarized this mission by saying that he had
not come to be served, but to serve, and to give his life as
a ransom for many (Mark 10.45). Consequently our
model for mission is that of a servant, and any church
which is to be true to its Master and Lord simply cannot
avoid going out of its way to become a servant too.

THE MANDATE TO THE CHURCH

> Go therefore and make disciples of all nations, bap-
> tizing them in the name of the Father and of the Son
> and of the Holy Spirit, teaching them to obey every-
> thing I have commanded you. And surely I am with
> you always, to the very end of the age.
>
> Matthew 28.19

Jesus's parting words as he ascended to heaven consti-
tute a tall order indeed: a commission to make disciples
from among all the nations. It is an order because at the
heart of it is a command to instill into the hearts of
Christians the same routine of witness that Jesus gave to
the apostles. We have already referred to the fact that all
these commissions have to do with proclaiming good
news and bringing the healing love to a range of needs
(Matthew 10.5–10; Luke 9.1–2; Acts 1.8). I particularly
want to refer to the parallel commission in Luke 10.1–9
because it adds the word 'others'. We are not told

whether those sent out were men or women, trained disciples or relative newcomers to the band that followed Jesus. They were simply available and willing to be sent and this is the model of true discipleship which is the pulse-beat of the Church.

The momentum of witness in the Gospels and Acts reveals a simple but compelling pattern. It began with individuals like John the Baptist and Jesus. Then it was shared with the twelve and by the time the Holy Spirit falls on the day of Pentecost 120 disciples are gathered to be sent out. The rest of the book of Acts is a focused survey of how mission spread out from Jerusalem to the surrounding areas of Judea and Samaria and then out to more distant nations. Adolf Harnack wrote that there is no doubt that the early church won all its victories by informal missionaries: they were spiritually contagious, they infected others with God.[4] To be called into relationship with Jesus is a challenge to discipleship and a commission to witness. To try to separate the two is like taking the beating heart out of a living person. The compelling truth is that every Christian is called to be a witness of their faith in Jesus Christ, and that not to be engaged in this is somehow to undermine the very fabric of that faith.

Consequently we should not be too surprised to find a return to mission in the Church because in doing this it is rediscovering its roots. I fully realize that this may sound like naïve optimism because not every church is engaged in mission and evangelism. However there are two factors we must not overlook. First, we are living in extraordinary days of renewal and in a moment we shall look at how renewal and evangelization are connected. Secondly, we are often too set in our ways when it comes to mission and evangelism. Therefore we need to examine our understanding of what in practice it means to bring good news to others and this forms the enquiry in the last part of this book.

SPIRITUAL RENEWAL

> You will receive power when the Holy Spirit comes
> upon you; and you will bear witness for me.
>
> Acts 1.8

The coming of the Holy Spirit usually results in the
Church going out. Jesus's mission began when the Holy
Spirit came upon him at his baptism. Jesus did battle
with the powers of darkness, he announced his commitment to proclaiming the Good News to the needy, he
healed the sick, and taught men and women how to live
a godly life. The gift of the Spirit was the spark as well as
the signal to engage in the works of God through evangelization. Little wonder, then, that in the days before
his crucifixion and resurrection Jesus devoted so much
of his teaching to the person of the Holy Spirit (John
14.15–27; 15.26–7; 16.5–15). Almost his last words before he leaves the disciples at his ascension are a command to be still and wait for the Holy Spirit to come;
then they would discover the impulse and power to be
witnesses (Luke 24.45–9).

Consequently, on the Day of Pentecost, the disciples
rediscovered their power to tell people about Jesus, the
Son of God, and to challenge them to repent and come
back to God. I say rediscovered because in their earlier
commissions they had been given a foretaste of the authority given to those born of the Spirit. The Holy Spirit
will always remind Christians that they have God's
power to change lives and circumstances. He also gives
us the authority which is not based on our own abilities
or on a holy lifestyle to witness to the fact that we too
have been brought into family relationship with God,
that we are his children (John 1.12).

My wife and I were visiting homes in our neighbourhood to share something of the gospel message. On one

occasion we were accompanied by Robbie, the local dustman who was just eighteen years old and had only recently given up his addiction to hard drugs. We called upon a retired school teacher who had taught scripture in Egypt and who, by his own profession, had no need of conversion to Christ. He recognized Robbie and was indignant that a local troublemaker should have the audacity to come to his door to tell him he needed Christ. He began to compare his many achievements in his long life with the apparently wasted life that Robbie had led so far. Needless to say, Robbie felt very intimidated by these many reminders of his faults and failings. Yet somewhere inside him the Holy Spirit stirred his heart and he simply replied to this harangue by saying, 'The only right I have is the one that Jesus has given me!'

The Spirit could not be contained in that upper room. By the very nature of God, the Holy Spirit drives us out into the arms of a society that has lost its way; only then can the world recognize its lostness and be reconnected with God through the saving love of Jesus Christ.

What is this mission?

At the heart of the Christian faith is the gospel or 'good news'. Mark opens his gospel account with the words 'The good news of Jesus Christ – the Message! – begins here.'[5] At once we are presented with the fact that the good news is Jesus himself. So however we may go about mission, it must have at its heart the invitation to know and experience the Lord Jesus Christ and to live as a disciple of the Son of God. Jesus is not only the message of good news, he is also its prime messenger. Mark writes that Jesus proclaimed the good news of God saying, 'the kingdom of God is near. Repent and believe the good news' (1.15).

WHAT IS MEANT BY GOOD NEWS?

This phrase 'good news' occurs seventy-two times in the New Testament: what does it mean?

The good news of God and Jesus

It is important to realize that this gospel revealed a God who was unlike any ever dreamed of in the New Testament world: a God who loved people enough to seek them out and offer them the good news that they could be saved. It also affirms that the whole initiative of the good news belongs with God. We must not be misled into thinking of an angry God and a gentle Christ and to imagine that what Jesus did on the cross changed the attitude of God. It was because God loved the world so much that he sent his Son to be our saviour.

If Jesus had not come into the world, there would be no good news to share. Jesus not only *told* people what God was like but he *showed* them the Father in his life and actions.

Good news for everyone

The Jewish people, who were the first to hear the good news, always believed that in God's order of things they were the favoured nation. But the good news is a gospel that knows no boundaries or favourites. It is good news for everyone.

THE CHALLENGE OF THE GOOD NEWS

Seeing that this good news originates with God and his plans for our world, there are certain challenges we must take to heart as a result.

It must be believed

The whole of the Christian life consists in living out life in the unshakeable conviction that the good news about Jesus is true. Without this conviction Christianity would be meaningless, which is why the life of the Church must reflect in every department that this good news has been taken to heart and that it shapes the lives of all its members.

It must be proclaimed
When someone finds the good news, they cannot be said to have found it in full until they want to share it with others. Christians cannot keep good news to themselves; every Christian is a missionary. It is a commonly accepted fact that the gospel message originally came to ancient Britain not by professional evangelists but by converted traders, Roman soldiers and slaves. To some degree as a nation we owe our Christian heritage to an anonymous collection of unknowns – ordinary people who were caught by the good news and could not help but share it wherever they went.

It is to be served
Receiving the good news is also a privilege and a duty. The lives of apostles and saints show us that they welcomed the call to pass on the good news whatever the risks may have been. I have recently been reading Thomas Cahill's book, *How the Irish Healed Civilization*.[6] It tells the story of how with the collapse of the Roman Empire and the onset of the Dark Ages, the Irish Celtic Church was virtually the sole Christian witness in Europe. Suffering appalling persecutions these Christians kept the good news and Christian education alive when there were no other people to do so. We too have a responsibility to let the light of our good news shine out to everyone and be prepared to serve in whatever capacity we are called and gifted.

WHAT IS THE GOOD NEWS?
Finally let us examine some of the ingredients of this good news and so build a picture of its importance and power.

The good news of truth
'With the coming of Jesus Christ the time of guesses about God is ended and the time of certainty begun.'[7] The Christian faith is light shining into our uncertainty and confusion, assuring us that God can be known through his Son Jesus Christ. I believe that there is definitely one thing which God has never wanted for the human race and that is insecurity. With the coming of the good news we can be confident that we are seeing and hearing the truth of our need for security and God's amazing love. 'Christianity was never meant to present us with a series of problems but with an armoury of certainties.'[8]

The good news of hope
John Buchan, the author of *The Thirty-Nine Steps*, defined an atheist as a person with no invisible means of support. When people realize what the good news means they are filled with hope for themselves and for the world. This is not an empty or romanticized hope in the face of the world's perplexing traumas and pains; the Christian gospel informs us that this is not the whole story and that at the end of every road we encounter the love and presence of God to heal and help us on. It is this hope which enables us to see the godly potential and meaning in every human being no matter how difficult and demanding they may be.

The good news of peace
The peace – shalom – of God brings us into wholeness of life and being. It is living apart from God that causes us to have a split personality and, therefore, in the words of Augustine, the fifth-century Bishop of Hippo, 'our hearts are restless until they find their rest in Thee'. The poet G. Studdard Kennedy, 'Woodbine Willie' to his admirers, once said that part of us comes from heaven and

the other from the earth. Heaven and earth come together again in the good news of Jesus Christ and we find peace of heart and mind. This peace comes from surrendering to God when we experience the death of a self-centred life and a rising to the new life of Christ within. It is this good news which brings us the possibility of a fully integrated personality, complete in the love of Christ.

Good news of immortality

I am challenged and fascinated by the account of the raising of Lazarus from the dead. Imagine the scene: Jesus is standing by the tomb at Bethany, listening to the grief, pain and anger of Martha and Mary. He weeps (John 11.35), he who is the resurrection and the life. Yet his tears are not because Lazarus is dead but because he is feeling the pain of death in his friends' lives; after all, he is a man of sorrows and acquainted with grief. It is after listening to the story of their bereavement that he creates the great miracle of restoring the dead man to life again. Yet this miracle is only minor in comparison with the marvellous miracle of eternal life. Even Lazarus grew older and at some later date died and went home to the Father's house for ever. You tell me which is the greater miracle? It is the promise of the good news that we shall be with Christ for ever and some day see him more clearly than this world at present allows. Consequently the death and resurrection of Jesus points the way in which we too will go and he is our constant companion every step of that journey.

Good news of salvation

It is good news because it heralds the fact that we are forgiven for our many sins past and present. Through the death of Christ upon the cross and by raising him to life again, God removes the guilt of our past and offers us the continual sustaining presence of his Holy Spirit to enable us to conquer sin and live in victory. Because of Jesus Christ we are made acceptable to God the Father and consequently we can come confidently into his love for us and tell him all our needs, knowing we will be heard.

The good news is a rich gift entrusted to the Church of Jesus Christ and by its very nature it impels us to go and share it with others. Furthermore, those who receive and live out this good news also receive healing to their lives, and this connection will be explored throughout this book.

2 Rediscovering the Healing Church

Until recently most people did not think of Christian healing as a mainstream ministry within the Church. A few clergy or laity were committed to it either because they had 'gifts' or because they felt a personal inclination towards it; but most of us were happy to leave it as a minority concern and relegate it to the fringe of our own thoughts and practice. Some Christians still think of it in this way – peripheral, a bit odd, something which can quite well be ignored if you do not happen to fancy it.

However a new perception of the importance of the healing ministry is rapidly coming into the Church and is doing so on a worldwide level. It was reflected by the Anglican bishops at the 1978 Lambeth Conference when they unanimously passed a three-part resolution affirming the ministry of healing.

The Conference praises God for the renewal of the ministry of healing within the churches in recent times and reaffirms:
1. that healing the sick in His name is as much part of the proclamation of the Kingdom as the preaching of the good news of Jesus Christ;
2. that to neglect this aspect of ministry is to diminish our part in Christ's total redemptive activity;
3. that the ministry to the sick should be an essential element in any revision of the liturgy.

Ten years later the 1988 Lambeth Conference expanded
this resolution into a three-page document. The language
is unequivocal. The bishops make it plain that they
regard Christian healing as a central and essential element
of normal church life: 'We urge all Bishops to encourage,
to oversee and to be themselves involved in the
ministry of healing in their dioceses', and '[we] declare
that the ministry of healing should be a regular part of
the ministry in every congregation.'

The biblical bases of healing

The bishops deserve attention in this not least because
they themselves have paid so much attention to the word
of Jesus. Jesus directed his followers both to preach and
heal. In fact he rarely referred to one without also referring
to the other. St Luke included a sort of mini-
handbook on Christian healing in chapters 8–10 of his
Gospel which shows this clearly.

Luke 8 is an account of a preaching and healing mission
which Jesus undertook personally. His preaching
about the kingdom of God attracted people from miles
around, and he demonstrated his place in that kingdom
by works of healing. A madman in a graveyard had his
sanity restored. A chronic twelve-year haemorrhage
cleared up. A little girl who was thought to be dead came
to life again.

The twelve disciples must have been astonished to see
it all, but I would guess that their astonishment must
have been even greater when they were sent out themselves
and told to undertake a preaching and healing
mission of their own. The command from Jesus was
'Preach the Kingdom of God and heal the sick' (Luke
9.2). We can imagine how bewildered and apprehensive
they would have felt as they went out with Christ's
words echoing in their ears; but as always, Jesus does not

give a command without also enabling his hearers to obey it, and so we are told that they 'travelled through all the villages, preaching the Good News and healing people everywhere' (Luke 9.6).

Maybe they were treated with a certain amount of awe themselves after this, but very soon Jesus made it very clear that neither the preaching nor the healing was to be restricted to the twelve. In Luke 10, seventy-two people were sent out ahead of Jesus to the towns and other places where he intended to go. 'Heal the sick,' he told them, 'and say to the people "The Kingdom of God has come near you." ' Again we can imagine their apprehension, but on this occasion too Jesus enabled them to fulfil the command and they were thrilled to report that even demons had obeyed them (Luke 10.17).

I am struck by the fact that the number seventy-two is a marvellously untidy one. Older Bible translations speak of the mission of the *seventy* and commentators thought that Jesus chose seventy people because there were thought to be seventy Gentile nations and it was his way of showing that Christianity was to go into the whole world. However modern translations overwhelmingly take the view that '*seventy two* were sent out in twos'. This number does not seem to symbolize anything – and for a very good reason. Jesus did not select the number seventy-two by premeditated design. He would probably have preferred a larger number, as he says: 'There is a large harvest but few workers to gather it in' (Luke 10.2). However seventy-two were available, and so seventy-two were sent out. Jesus used the people who were on offer – and he still does.

The Church's healing ministry

The letter of James presents a picture of the ministry of healing in the life of an ordinary Christian congregation in the early Chuch:

Is anyone ill? He should send for the church elders who will pray for him and anoint him in the name of the Lord. This prayer made in faith will heal the sick person, the Lord will restore him to health and the sins he has committed will be forgiven. So then confess your sins to one another and pray for one another, so that you will be healed.

(James 5.14–16)

It was clearly understood in New Testament times that Jesus had given a general commission to his Church to preach and heal, and that this commission was not withdrawn. So why has healing not been a natural and integral element in the life of every congregation throughout the history of the Church? Why has it had to be rediscovered?

The late Revd George Bennett used to argue that the Emperor Constantine had much to do with the loss of this ministry. Before Constantine Christianity had been an illegal religion in the Roman Empire, and nobody would have claimed to be a Christian unless motivated by a real and deep belief. But when Constantine became a Christian early in the fourth century the days of persecution came to an end. According to Bennett's theory people then started going to church because it was the respectable thing to do and this may well have resulted in a decline in the spirituality of many claiming to be Christians. The decline would have continued at the end of the fourth century when Emperor Theodosius instituted penalties for *not* being a Christian.

This dealt a body-blow to the Christian healing ministry. Preaching could be undertaken by anyone, regardless of their spirituality, but *healing could not*. The doctrine of 'dispensationalism' was conceived which taught that the command to preach was given for ever but the command to heal was meant to apply only to the earliest years in the life of the Christian Church. There is clearly no basis for this in Scripture, but it accounted for the drop in the number of healings which were being reported.

That was a long time ago, however. The question remains – why has it taken *us* so long to rediscover the ministry of Christian healing in our own day with all the emphasis which we now place on the study of the Bible? Or to put it personally, why did it take *me* so long to rediscover Christian healing in my own life and ministry?

Perhaps the answer is that though the *authority* for the Church to have a healing ministry is clear, because it goes back to the command of Jesus, the *resources* on which we are to rely are less clear. When we go to the doctor's surgery, his resources are very evident. There on his desk is his prescription pad, giving us access to countless products of the drugs companies and, if necessary, he can refer us to a well-equipped hospital. By contrast the resources available at Christian healing services are less apparent. So church leaders can feel very nervous of taking the risk of starting them. Yet resources there certainly are and it is not too difficult to see what they are once we begin to think seriously about the question.

We need to remember that we have from Jesus not only a command but a promise. One of the most important texts in the Bible to help us understand the resources of the Christian healing ministry is Christ's pledge that 'where two or three are gathered together in my name, there am I in the midst of them' (Matthew 18.20). Christian worship is not a commemoration of a dead hero but a meeting with a living Lord. During Jesus's earthly ministry he was involved in one healing after another. It was as though he could not help himself. People were changed in his presence and discovered new levels of wholeness of body, mind and spirit. So if we truly meet him in worship, we should not be surprised if that meeting has healing implications. Logically we ought to be much more surprised if healing never took place.

Then where God the Son is present, God the Father cannot be absent. Jesus said 'I and my Father are one' (John 10.30), and 'He who has seen me has seen the Father' (John 14.9). If we worship in the name and in the presence of Jesus, it is the Christian conviction that we cannot help but make genuine contact with God the Father. If we accept this, once again simple logic points to the healing potential of worship. 'In the beginning God created' (Genesis 1.1). The Father's essence is creativity and when creativity meets that which is damaged the result is likely to be '*re-creativity*' or healing. So if we truly experience the Creator in worship, we should not be surprised if worship proves to be *re-creative* at every level of our being.

In the words of the Nicene Creed God the Holy Spirit 'proceeds from the Father and the Son' and he is 'the Lord and giver of life'. When we pray to the Father through the Son we should expect the Holy Spirit to move within us, nudging aside everything that is alien to God's plan and purpose for us and creating new life in body, mind and spirit. Belief in healing follows on from this.

The resources of Christian healing are therefore no less than those of God the Father, God the Son and God the Holy Spirit. These resources could not be more orthodox or more powerful. By comparison even the best products of the drug companies surely pale into insignificance as a resource for healing. The Church has always claimed to believe in the Trinity. It is now high time for us to recognize that this belief is no mere academic doctrine: it has startling implications. It is also time to research and rediscover these implications within the practice of the Christian healing ministry.

I believe that the life of every ordinary church should provide a series of channels through which the healing power of God the Father, God the Son, and God the Holy Spirit can flow. Anything else is irrelevant to our purpose as the body of Christ.

What is Christian healing?

The time has come for a precise definition of Christian healing, and it is difficult to improve on that offered by Bishop Morris Maddocks: 'Christian Healing is Jesus Christ meeting us at our point of need.'[1] When Jesus meets us with all the might of his oneness with the Father and the Holy Spirit, the encounter will never be a non-event. Things will happen. Jesus will make a difference and this difference is the essence of Christian healing. It extends to every aspect of life, affecting our bodies, minds and spirits, our attitudes, relationships and life-styles. It affects us as individuals, it affects us in society, and it will affect us as a nation if we give Christ half a chance. It is relevant to our experience on earth and it transforms our prospects for eternity.

Later in this book we will look at some of the channels of Christian healing which should characterize the life of the Church. We will look at healing services, the deliverance ministry, and baptismal ministry, as well as ministry connected with marriage, funeral services and bereavement support, parish missions, and some of the distinctive forms of ministry required by different age groups. We will see them all as channels of Christian healing, but in doing so we will not come anywhere near exhausting the potential which ordinary church life can have for channelling the healing power of Jesus.

Anything at all which communicates the reality of Jesus Christ personally to you and me will be a channel of Christian healing as far as we are concerned. All sorts of things can serve as 'mini-sacraments'; these have no power in themselves, but if they help some individual to practise the presence of Jesus, they are not to be mocked or rejected as superstitious. For instance the Bible tells us that St Paul's handkerchiefs and aprons were used as channels of Christian healing for some people (Acts 19.12). There was nothing magic about them but the handkerchiefs and aprons would have reminded people of Paul and Paul reminded people of Jesus and so Jesus made a difference: 'God performed unusual miracles' and 'diseases were driven away'.

Have you ever heard of healing by carpets? I imagine not, and yet in my last parish when visiting the home of two members of my congregation I was never allowed to stand on a certain part of the sitting-room carpet. 'That's a holy place', they said. They had greatly benefitted from the prayers of a former curate and their 'holy place' was the spot where he always knelt to pray when he visited their home. The carpet reminded them of their friend the curate and he in his turn reminded them of Jesus. In times of trouble they would kneel in just the same place and for them it was a channel of Christian healing, a means by which Jesus made a difference.

Not only worship but social occasions too should have a potential for healing, whether we think of the clatter of coffee cups after a service or occasions such as a harvest supper or a parish Christmas party, because Christian social life should be an expression of Christian love with all its healing implications. Even administrative meetings of bodies like Parochial Church Councils can have healing in them. Such meetings do not have to be dull or routine, particularly if the discussion ranges over the whole life of the church and community and asks the questions 'What would Jesus say?' and 'What would Jesus do?' In the course of my ministry I have experienced Church Council meetings at their worst and at their best. There is all the difference in the world. I used to dread them, but now I can look forward to them and feel the healing power of Jesus working through them.

I believe in the rediscovery of Christian healing ministry in the life of ordinary churches for many reasons: the authority for it is a command from the highest level; its resources are mighty beyond measure; and the channels are so many that when I attempt to list them I never come to an end. This ministry is true to Scripture, and it is also true to reason, so far as reason goes.

We know that a bad experience, a negative thought, a wrong attitude can act like a poison and harm us physically as well as mentally and spiritually. For instance a festering grudge can damage us physically in a wide range of ways ranging from stopping us sleeping and spoiling our appetite to making us feel physically unwell. On the other hand a good experience, a positive attitude can act like the best of medicines. Psychologists tell us that from the earliest days of our lives loving relationships are a source of health and happiness, so logically what could be better for us at every level of our being than a loving relationship with the Son of God himself?

Perhaps personally I need rather less faith these days to accept the healing power of Christ because I have now seen it in action so many times. It is not like a magic wand, and I would not like to give the impression that the Christian healing ministry produces guaranteed automatic cures. I wrestle continually with all sorts of problems within this ministry. I can become baffled with life and angry with God when I yearn for a result that does not come. Yet time and time again I have seen just what Jesus can do.

There was Jim in hospital with broken ribs, double pneumonia, and a dangerously high temperature. The sweat ran down him in little rivulets, and yet after a laying on of hands with prayer his temperature instantly reverted to normal to the astonishment of his nurse and he went on to make a steady recovery. There was Gladys whose arthritis caused her considerable distress, yet she was free from it for ten years after attending a healing service. Then she developed depression and diverticulitis and so I went to her house and her husband and I laid hands on her with prayer for her healing. The next day, they came to the vicarage to tell me that her diverticulitis had improved out of all recognition and that her depression had vanished. There was Joanne whose agoraphobia left her after she received the ministry of Christian healing. Bill and Ben were atheists, who both wrote to me to tell me how faith returned to them as they watched a healing service from our church on television.

I should add that neither I nor any of my colleagues at St Stephen's and St Alban's in Prenton are aware of having any special personal 'gift' of healing other than the gift of the presence of Jesus who promised his followers 'I will be with you always to the end of time' (Matthew 28.20). The fulfilment of that promise is all we need. My belief is that every local church is called to be a healing church because we are the body of Christ. Jesus healed because it was his nature, and if we are his body we should be a healing church for the same reason.

Let St Teresa put it all into perspective for us with her famous words: 'Christ has no body now on earth but yours, no hands but yours, no feet but yours. Yours are the eyes through which his compassion must look on the world. Yours are the feet with which he must go about doing good. Yours are the hands with which he must bless men now.' Martin Luther taught simply that the Christian is called to be a Christ to his neighbour. Then there are the amazing words of Jesus himself which stretch our faith to the limit: 'whoever believes in me will do the things that I do – and even greater things!' (John 14.12).

3 Is There a Connection between Healing and Evangelism?

The Gospel connection with Jesus's mission

It is a remarkable fact that the commissions which Jesus gave to his disciples include both to proclaim the good news and to pray for healing. These form the cohesive and inseparable core of our gospel mission, as we see from Luke's account of the sending out of the twelve:

> He gave them power and authority to drive out all demons and to cure diseases, and he sent them out to preach the kingdom of God and to heal the sick.
>
> Luke 9.1–2

The mission of Jesus himself is the model for this balance of healing and preaching the kingdom of God.

· Matthew introduces the public ministry of Jesus as taking the dual form of preaching the good news in the synagogues and healing every disease and sickness among the people (Matthew 4.23). Just as the gift of salvation is for all people, so the healing ministry of Jesus addresses 'every' disease and sickness. It might even be said that Matthew models the whole of his gospel narrative on the connection between evangelization and healing. He presents the teaching ministry of Jesus in a series of blocks which are interspersed with accounts of his healing ministry. While the other three Gospels do not present their material in quite the same fashion as

Matthew, they nonetheless reveal Jesus who announces good news of salvation and meets people's needs in healing. We do a disservice to the community and weaken the gospel message if we attempt to untie the threefold cord of mission – teaching, healing and proclaiming the good news – and concentrate on just one of its parts.

This was brought home to me very forcibly and painfully when, as an assistant Baptist minister, I took part in a pioneer outreach on a new council estate in Birkenhead. The speaker insisted on calling the mission a divine healing crusade. I argued for calling it a divine healing and gospel mission but the change of name turned out to be only a cosmetic exercise as the speaker concentrated on the subject of healing. Over 700 people came forward for prayer for healing and were all subsequently seen by members of our counselling team. However, we were greatly disappointed when it came to visiting these people and inviting them to attend the new church we were hoping to establish in the wake of the mission. They were not really interested in a committed faith nor in belonging to a church: they had come for healing and not much else. I am convinced that this was the result of dividing up the good news and omitting proper reference to the challenge to turn one's life over to Jesus Christ as Lord and Saviour.

The ministry of Jesus

> Jesus – the name that charms our fears,
> That bids our sorrows cease;
> 'Tis music in the sinner's ears,
> 'Tis LIFE and HEALTH, and PEACE.
>
> Charles Wesley (1707–88)

We shall now examine in more detail the benefits to us of Jesus's ministry and in the process see where healing and evangelization meet in the life and experience of the believer.

THE GOSPEL CONNECTION WITH LIFE

> I have come that they may have life, and have it to the full.

> John 10.10

The good news shows that God's promise of a new quality of life is only possible through a personal relationship with Jesus Christ. One of the major themes of the New Testament is the victory of life over death. It is because of our sin and self-centredness that we shall die and it is this path of self-destruction that Jesus challenges when he says, 'I tell you the truth, whoever hears my word and believes in him who sent me has eternal life and will not be condemned; he has crossed over from death to life' (John 5.24).

Jesus is the source of life for he has life in himself (John 5.26); all other life is derived from him. This is reinforced at the beginning of John's Gospel where Jesus is revealed as the active agent in creation and the source of all life in the universe (John 1.3–4). Consequently Jesus is both the source for life itself here and also the resource for living life to the full on earth. Paul sums this up when he says 'The life I live in the body, I live by the faith of the Son of God who loved me and gave himself for me' (Galations 2.20). The gospel message is the promise of life which stretches beyond the confines of time, and our own resurrection, following a trail already blazed by Jesus Christ who first rose from the dead. In his classic treatise on resurrection to immortality, Paul describes Jesus as the first fruits of this reality, the foretaste of what God has in store for every believer, and this is why he can triumphantly send out the challenge

'Where, O death, is your victory? Where, O death, is your sting?' (1 Corinthians 15.55).

Eternal life involves much more than immortality, however. 'It is the quality of eternity unlimited by time.'[1] This is certainly what Jesus meant when he described the life he offered others as life 'in all its fullness' (John 10.10, New English Bible). It is in fact the quality of God's life that Jesus came to bring us. Here we have our connection with health and healing, for health has been defined as the fulness and completeness of life. Nothing could be healthier than the life of God in a person, producing in him or her the wholeness, soundness and righteousness which constitutes true health and holiness.

Yet this quality of godly living is not given as a package for us to open and apply to our lives; it breathes out from a living relationship with Jesus Christ as Lord. When I was a young pastor I used to walk home one of the very elderly ladies in the church. She walked slowly and with the aid of a stick. One day, as we were going along, a young man with very long hair and an equally large beard came towards us. As he came up to us he stepped off the pavement in a bid to pass us by. It was at this moment that Annie swapped her walking stick to her other hand and held it out, blocking the young man's passage. He seemed very annoyed and I was not a little worried about what he was going to say or do. At this point Annie said to the man, 'I have watched you walk by a lot of times but there is something I really want to tell you.' He stood still and in a sarcastic voice said, 'What's that then?' Annie said, 'You look just like Jesus!' He was a little shocked but obviously pleased because he broke into a smile and stroked his hair at the same time saying, 'Do I really?' 'Yes,' Annie replied, 'now live like him!' The stunned look of recognition on his face as the gospel penny dropped was a picture to see. The actual life which the good news announces is none other than living like Jesus, with the power of the Holy Spirit to help us translate his life into practice in every aspect of our lives. Salvation and healing are therefore a life which is lived in response to the gospel challenge to stop living apart and independently from God.

THE GOSPEL CONNECTION WITH HEALTH

'Was no one found to return and give praise to God save this foreigner?' Then he said to him, 'Rise and go; your faith has made you well.'

Luke 17.19

At the heart of the word used in the New Testament for salvation ('sozo') is the idea of soundness or health. Luke, the physician, uses it to highlight the interplay between salvation and healing, and describes two healing stories which bring these themes into sharp relief. They are the account of the woman with twelve years' bleeding (Luke 8.42–8) and the ten lepers who were healed (Luke 17.11–19). In both accounts Luke, when speaking of their healing, uses a familiar word from his knowledge of the medical world for 'cure' or 'restoring to health'. However, there is a deeper and more complete healing which still needed to take place in their lives. The woman in the crowd responds to Jesus's request that she acknowledge who she is: she comes and kneels before him in worship and confession and tells all that was in her heart. The tenth leper is full of joy and praise to God for his cure and willingly runs back to Jesus to worship at his feet. Both healed people were acknowledging their gratitude for healing and their personal need of Jesus. It was this latter motivation that brought about their greater healing, that of being made whole, 'safe and sound' in the salvation of God. Nine lepers were only healed but the tenth was made whole!

The healing of physical disease served to point the way to a more complete therapy for the human condition, that of personal salvation. So John describes some of Jesus's healings as signs. They are signals of the saving power of God which is active in the world now as well as an indication of the more complete healing which will come to the redeemed when the Son of God returns in his glory. There are four healings which John calls signs: the healing of the official's son (4.46–54), the healing at the Pool of Bethesda (5.15), the man born blind (9.1–41) and the raising of Lazarus (11.1–44).

The healing of the official's son (John 4.46–54)

It is interesting to note the rebuke in John 4.48 where Jesus says, 'Unless you people see miraculous signs and wonders you will never believe.' This is not a deterrent to the healing ministry; it is a challenge not to be more concerned with physical healings than with the whole salvation of God. How we need this balance in the healing ministry today! It is apparent that the official in the story remembered Jesus's words because when he discovered that his son was healed he and his entire household became Christians. In other words, this healing had had its desired effects: it pointed the beneficiaries to the love of God and they were made whole in that love because they trusted in Jesus as Lord.

The healing at the Pool of Bethesda (John 5.15)

'Here was not just a man with a sickness but a sick man.'[2] Here was a man who had had a chronic illness for thirty-eight years. Jesus asks him a question which he asked no one else and it was 'Do you want to get well?' It is this question which shows that his need went far beyond a mere curing of his illness. It seems that he clung to his illness in a dependent and unhealthy way and his evasive answer seems to corroborate this. He replied, 'I have no one to help me.' When Jesus healed him he was at the same time challenging the man's will to live a new life in harmony with God. In fact this man, now healed, is later found in the temple, presumably worshipping God and offering thanks for his healing. Jesus still addresses the deeper healing of making him 'safe and sound' when he says, 'See, you are well again. Stop sinning or something worse may happen to you' (v.14). So physical healing falls short if it does not connect with a healing of heart wherein Jesus is acknowledged as Lord.

Each of the healings makes it clear that the good news of Jesus is health to body and soul. The essence of this health is knowing the love of Christ and believing in him; it means that all other healings, however important, are intended to lead us to embrace this love of Christ and, by his Spirit, to live like him in the world.

The healing of blind Bartimaeus is a good concluding example for this section. Here is a man whose healing is linked to his confession of commitment to Jesus. Twice he hails Jesus in messianic terms as 'Son of David' and once cured, he completes his healing by being a follower of Jesus (Mark 10.46–52).

THE GOSPEL CONNECTION WITH PEACE

> Peace I leave with you; my peace I give you.
> Do not let your hearts be troubled and do
> not be afraid.

John 14.27

It is a commonplace to say that we live in a troubled and violent world, but the need for peace of heart and mind has always been an elusive and much sought-after commodity. In our advanced society, where we can send machines deep into space and store vast amounts of information in a microchip, it remains a struggle to find inner peace and to achieve unity in human relationships. It is no surprise therefore that the scriptural revelation paints a picture of a God of peace who goes out of his way at Calvary to bring his peace to our world and lives.

The Hebrew concept of peace is shalom and the word conveys the image of wholeness, unity and harmony. There is the idea of blessedness, health and fulfilment that comes essentially from a relationship with God. Hence the Messiah is the Prince of Peace who will bring wholeness to the individual and in time put an end to wars (Isaiah 9.1–7). In the Old Testament the man of faith is the one who fixes his thoughts on God and so gains inner wholeness and a confidence in God to keep him safe through all the ups and downs of life (Psalms 4.8; 119.165). It is the wicked man who has no peace because he attempts to live apart from God's presence (Isaiah 57.20–1).

Jesus is the evangelist of peace, who preached peace to those far off and to those who were near (Ephesians 2.17). The good news is good news because it restores us to a loving relationship with God which as far as God was concerned never stopped, but was interrupted and shattered by human sinfulness. Our relationship with God is healed through the gift of salvation in Jesus Christ and we find true inner peace.

A good example of this is the healing of the severely demonized man whom Jesus met when he crossed the lake of Galilee for a time of peace and quiet (Luke 8.26–39). After the demons have been cast out and his neighbours have come to see what had happened, he is described as 'sitting at Jesus's feet, dressed and in his right mind' (v.35). Here is peace with God whereby we are sitting before Jesus as his disciple, restored, healed and forgiven. Peace for this troubled man was not only having the evil driven out of him but also being restored to wholeness and harmony in the presence of Jesus Christ. And his peace, his 'shalom', is evangelistic because he goes on his way announcing the good news of how much the Christ had done for him. Peace cannot be kept as a private possession. It has to be shared or it dissipates.

The peace of God, therefore, is multi-relational. It heals our relationship with God which is the first instalment of salvation. It also heals our relationship with ourselves which can be described as our journey of healing and wholeness. Very often it is the love and acceptance of God which enables us to go on and begin to accept and love ourselves as we are. This is not a commitment to self-indulgence but a challenge to grow in holiness in Christ. There are so many Christians who have been wounded and abused through their journey in life and lay the blame at their own doors. Others are aware of the wrong they have done and find it hard to accept themselves and receive forgiveness. But once we have received God's love and forgiveness and find not punishment or blame but the beauty of his peace, we are then encouraged and energized to open our hearts to inner healing. The healing of salvation is an invitation to further and more personal healing.

The peace of God also extends to the healing of our relationship with others. The apostle Paul beautifully portrays peace as it is experienced by the believing community living in fellowship with the Lord:

As God's chosen people, holy and dearly loved, clothe yourselves with compassion, kindness, humility, gentleness and patience. Bear with each other and forgive whatever grievances you may have against one another. Forgive as the Lord forgave you. And over all these virtues put on love, which binds them all together in perfect unity. Let the peace of Christ rule in your hearts, since as members of one body you were called to peace.

Colossians 3.12–15

This pilgrimage of healing and salvation is not a lonely journey but a shared one.

Finally, the peace of God will come on earth and there will be healing in communities and between nations. The fellowship of the Church is also a sign and a sacrament for this. John in the Book of Revelation links the healing of the new community of the Church, the new Jerusalem, with the outpouring of a river of life from its midst which will bring healing to the nations (Revelation 21.1–4; 22.1–2). This is not too dissimilar to the vision of Isaiah who saw a restored and healed Israel as the focus for the gathering of the nations who seek to live at peace with God and their neighbours (Isaiah 2.1–4). God's shalom is therefore a call to salvation which results in healed relationships within ourselves and within the community of Christians; and it leads us to witness our wider communities and nations, where the reign of God's peace is yet to come.

We have been looking at the woven cord of the good news and have discovered that it intertwines proclaiming the message of salvation and the healing of lives. Therefore when we engage in mission we must not neglect the whole commission of our Lord Jesus Christ. We cannot break it down into compartments, whereby we may on one occasion preach the gospel and on another address the subject of healing. We are living at a time when God is renewing his Church and challenging it to declare his loving intentions towards us. I hope my co-author will forgive me for quoting something he once told me. Everything his church engages in, in order to be truly sound, must, he said, have a healing benefit to his people and community. This is the true gospel connection.

4 A Service of Healing – and Evangelism

If healing is central to the Scriptures it follows that it should have a central place in our worship. This conclusion seemed to me inescapable once I had spent some time researching the place of Christian healing in the Bible, in Christian tradition, and in the current experience of the Church. This chapter is a description of the type of healing service which has evolved as a basic ingredient in my own ministry after that time of study.

Healing is a major biblical topic; indeed it is no exaggeration to say that the Bible is a book about healing. Its concern is for the healing of the total person and of the society in which he or she lives.

At the beginning of Genesis God reveals himself as Creator. Then when creation has been damaged by man's folly and sin, he reveals himself as Re-creator. He says to the Israelites, 'I am the Lord, the one who heals you' (Exodus 15.26). The psalms, the Book of Proverbs and the prophets all have their healing message, and it is no surprise to find that since Jesus came into this world to do the will of his Father (John 6.38) healing was an essential element in his life and ministry. There were many individual healings: blindness (Matthew 9.27–31), deafness (Mark 7.31–5), lameness (Matthew 11.4–5), paralysis (Matthew 8.5–13), fever (Matthew 8.14–15), skin conditions (Matthew 8.1–3) and so on. There were mass healings, as in Matthew 14.14. Also Jesus made it plain, as we have seen in Luke 9.1–6 and 10.1–9, that it was his will to continue his healing ministry through his Church.

In my case it all started as a piece of academic research as I studied text after text in the Bible and then went on to consider the place of healing in the teaching and ministry of some of the early Fathers and their successors. But ultimately I had to face the question, what about me? What about my own ministry, my own church?

There were various possibilities. One was to leave these thoughts in the realm of the academic, write a thesis, get it out of my system and forget it in practical terms. It was tempting, but it would have been dishonest. Alternatively I could keep Christian healing as a low-key periodic element in my personal pastoral ministry, but not refer to it publicly and not include it in corporate worship. Then if it should go wrong not many people would notice. It was tempting, but it would have been cowardly.

Another possibility was to gather a like-minded group and start a small mid-week meeting for healing prayer. But if healing is central in the Scriptures and central in the mind and the ministry of Christ, it would have been less than obedient to tuck it away in a corner of church life. So I was left with no option but to introduce the theme of Christian healing into the mainstream of my church's worship at a regular Sunday service, and I have now been conducting these services for more than twenty years.

To begin with I was very cautious. I did not dare use the words 'healing service' but talked instead about services which 'investigated Christian healing' or 'sought to rediscover Christian healing'. Then slowly I came to the point where I found myself able to talk about 'Christian healing services' and even to advertise them on the notice board outside the church.

In my present parish we hold a healing service in the parish church on the third Sunday of every month and in our daughter church on the first Sunday of every month. These services have become very precious to us. We learn and experience many things as they take place month by month. They influence every part of our parish life. People often travel many miles to attend them. As adviser in the healing ministry to the Bishop of Chester I have helped other parishes to start these services and personally I cannot now conceive of a full ministry without them.

The form of service

When people attend one of our healing services for the first time, they are handed a leaflet explaining what we do and why we do it. This leaflet explains what will happen during the service and includes a couple of prayers: one offering ourselves for healing and the other responding to Jesus as our Saviour and Lord.

Our healing service was originally based on a modified version of the 1662 prayerbook Evensong. Now we use ASB Evening Prayer, with a new musical setting of the versicles and responses. This includes some guitar music alongside the more traditional music of the organ and choir. Personally I prefer Evensong to Holy Communion as the setting for a Church of England Christian healing service. This is because I believe that the Church is called to rediscover Holy Communion for its own sake. There is such depth and truth and power in it that it strikes me as almost impertinent to do anything other than receive it with gratitude and value it for its own sake.

By contrast Evensong is a slender little service. It can easily accommodate special concerns and readily becomes a vehicle for rediscovering the ministry of Christian healing. I also prefer it to any specially designed form of healing service, because by using an ordinary form of worship we make it easier for the healing service to act as a bridge to other services, and that is in fact what has happened in our experience in Prenton. Similarly, when a healing service is taking place within a Christian tradition other than the Church of England, I believe that the normal denominational pattern of evening worship should be retained.

When I arrived in Prenton twenty years ago there was no evening worship at our daughter church, St Alban's, and Evensong at the parish church, St Stephen's, was ailing. It was attended by about a dozen in the congregation plus a small choir and we were wondering whether to abolish it and concentrate on the mid-morning Parish Communion service, as a number of other churches have done.

About thirty people attended the first of our monthly Christian healing services and gradually, month by month, the number increased, with the result that now over a hundred people may attend. It was noticeable that the healing service was giving the kiss of life to all our other evening services. Now there is certainly no thought of abolishing evening worship. Before long members of St Alban's asked that they too might have their own Christian healing service one Sunday evening a month. So we now have a healing service at St Alban's on the first Sunday of each month as well as one at St Stephen's on the third Sunday.

We continually notice new faces at both these services. It did not take us long to discover that our healing service is a natural vehicle for evangelism. There is something very special in the atmosphere which makes this so. It has nothing to do with emotionalism; Church of England Evensong is hardly an emotional rave-up. Yet there is in the atmosphere both a sense of need and a sense of expectancy. Of course this must not be exploited, but because we seek to respond to need in an honest and scriptural way, it happens time and time again that I find myself directing the congregation at this service to the simple facts of the gospel, because it is these which are the heart of our resource for healing.

Another reason why a Christian healing service seems to have a distinct evangelistic power lies in the high quality of the prayer content. It is often so tangible that people are able to feel it when they come in. It is not just that some are following the advice of the preparatory leaflet confessing fears and anxieties to God, and opening themselves to God's forgiveness and cleansing. At St Stephen's we have a dozen or so people who meet in our side-chapel for half an hour before the service, praying for the healing of the world. A member of the congregation has made it her responsibility to prepare a leaflet every month setting out the hurts and needs of a different area, so that we can bring them to the Lord of healing.

The atmosphere of prayer does not prevent our seeking to offer a sensitive and warm welcome to new-comers when they enter the church. It is important that they are made to feel at ease and at home. It is for the same reason that page numbers are given out and that there is an occasional pause in the service for explanation and comment, so that even those who are totally unaccustomed to Church of England liturgy can be at ease and relax into the spirit of worship.

Preaching and healing

The sermon plays a vitally important part in a healing service, just as it does in an evangelistic service, and the aim of the sermon in each case is very similar.

I remember the vicar of the church in which I served my curacy telling me of an occasion on which he had been invited to preach in a prestigious city-centre church. He was an able preacher and he had prepared a suitably erudite sermon. He mounted the pulpit clutching his sermon notes, ready to demonstrate his impressive preaching talents. Then as he stood waiting for the hymn before the sermon to come to an end he noticed a brass plaque in front of him with a single text – John 12.21 – 'Sir, we would see Jesus'. Suddenly he felt rather ashamed. He put aside his sermon notes and quietly and simply started to speak of how he saw Jesus and of what Jesus meant to him. Afterwards he was told he had preached one of the finest sermons of his life!

There could be no better text than this to guide any preacher at a healing service or an evangelistic service. In each case the preacher should be seeing Jesus and helping others to see him equally clearly. Then Jesus will do his own work of healing and evangelism. The preacher's main task is not to get in his way.

When regular healing services are introduced into the life of a church, it seems best to begin with a short series of sermons on the basic principles of Christian healing, but then as soon as possible to leave these introductory sermons behind and to embark upon systematic Bible study based on one of the Gospels. In St Stephen's, Prenton I have now preached through the whole of St Luke's Gospel, chapter by chapter, leaving nothing out, followed by the whole of the Acts of the Apostles and St Paul's letters to the Corinthians. Currently we are studying St Matthew's Gospel. At St Alban's we have made our way through the whole of St Mark's Gospel and are now journeying through St John's, chapter by chapter. In every sermon the Bible itself has selected my subject for me and I have never found it to be irrelevant to the quest to see Jesus clearly and to understand the healing difference which it is his will to make to life.

I know of no way of presenting the reality of Jesus which does not involve an explicit or implicit challenge to respond to him. Any specifically Christian healing service should present this challenge, and the laying on of hands which in our service follows the sermon provides a natural and non-embarrassing way for members of the congregation to make a positive response.

It is not difficult to make this ministry available within the life of an ordinary church. No special 'gifts' are needed. Our practice is to minister in pairs, with each pair usually consisting of a member of staff and a member of the congregation. On the basis that Jesus said 'Those who believe shall lay hands on the sick' (Mark 16.18), I feel able to invite any member of the congregation to be a ministrant providing he or she believes in Jesus as Lord and Saviour, believes in the historical truth of the healing ministry of Jesus, and accepts the validity of its continuation within the Church, the body of Christ, today. Our ministrants lay hands on each other first and then offer the same ministry to all comers. It is a simple procedure, with a prayer which each pair say in unison: 'May the healing power of the Holy Spirit be in you.' Though our voices and our hands are used, we do not regard ourselves as 'healers'. There is only one Healer present – Jesus. It is because we are his body that we can offer his touch, just as it is because I am part of his body that I can preach his word.

Why seek healing?

In our experience most people want to come forward for the laying on of hands when given the opportunity. This is true of our services in Prenton and of the many services which I have conducted around Britain and overseas.

Most of us know instinctively that we need the touch of the Lord. Even if our physical health is excellent, we may well be able to identify other areas of our life and our lifestyle which badly need Christ's touch. We may also understand that the laying on of hands provides an opportunity to pray in a special way for someone we love, or we may use it as an opportunity to bring his cleansing influence into our relationships in a new way. We may want to use it to strengthen or even to start a relationship with Jesus himself. Possibly we may not altogether know why we want to come forward. But just as we would want to reach out and touch Jesus if he were to walk down the aisle of the church, so also it seems natural to want a laying on of hands in his name, even without a specific reason.

It is our practice never to ask those who come forward why they have done so. Personally I believe that to ask 'Why have you come?' or 'What is the matter?' or 'What would you like us to pray for?' can stop many people from coming forward. They may have an embarrassing problem (like a venereal disease or a menstrual problem or haemorrhoids) that they could not bring themselves to mention. Their problem might be so complex (a nervous breakdown, a phobia, a suicidal urge) that there is no way it could be expressed in a few words. Perhaps they are not at all sure what their problem is; they may not know why they feel depressed or anxious or unfulfilled. But because Christ knows and wants to meet us at our point of need, the most important thing we can do at a Christian healing service is to practise his presence and wait for him to act. A lady once said to me, 'When I knelt at the communion rail receiving the laying on of hands, I found I couldn't remember why I had come forward. Does that mean it won't work?' I was able to tell her that that probably meant it had already started to work!

The laying on of hands

The practice of laying hands on people, as described in this chapter, is of course only one out of many possibilities. For my own part I prefer it for several reasons. It encourages those who need it to come forward (provided that the invitation is wide-ranging and no personal questions are asked). It involves members of the congregation as ministrants so that this is seen to be a 'ministry of the body' not a star turn by some spiritual specialist. It helps a congregation to develop a sense of need and a sense of responsibility.

Its symbolism is profoundly evangelistic. Offering of the touch of Christ symbolizes his presence, his availability, and his relevance. He is the Saviour who can make all the difference in the world to us. He is the Father's greatest gift, the bargain offer of all time and beyond all time. But there is no message of automatic salvation in the Christian Faith: God will not thrust himself upon us. We need to respond (hence the symbolism of getting up and coming forward) and we need to do so in a spirit of humble availability (hence the symbolism of kneeling).

Perhaps a word should be said about the concept of receiving on behalf of someone else. Some Christians find difficulty in this. I heard some time ago of a doctor who stormed out of a Parochial Church Council discussion on the ministry of Christian healing when the possibility of receiving 'by proxy' was mentioned. To him it smacked of superstition and mumbo jumbo. Yet I am sure that the same doctor must have prayed on many an occasion for an absent patient or friend. Receiving a laying on of hands for an absent friend is just a way of praying – but it is a powerful way of praying.

Some years ago we were delighted to hear of an American woman whose double vision cleared up in the United States when her friends in Prenton received the laying on of hands on her behalf. Sometime later she came to England and gave her testimony at St Stephen's to the healing she had received through our long-distance ministry.

More recently another woman approached me after I had spoken at a meeting in her parish. She said, 'I think I should tell you that I believe you have saved my life.' I was puzzled because we had never met, but she explained that some months earlier she had been seriously ill in hospital. She was comatose and it seemed that life was slipping away from her. Then one Sunday, to the amazement of her doctors and nurses, she sat up in bed and extensive tests showed that inexplicably there was nothing wrong with her. It happened to be the same Sunday when one of her close friends came to our healing service in Prenton and received a laying on of hands on her behalf. It could be a coincidence, but I am reminded of the words attributed to Archbishop William Temple: 'I find that when I pray coincidences happen, and when I stop praying coincidences stop happening!'

I was sad to hear of the doctor who walked out of his PCC when the ministry of healing was discussed; but for that one doctor I know of dozens more who are completely committed to the Christian healing ministry. We often have medical personnel (doctors, physiotherapists, nurses) taking part in the laying on of hands at our healing services and neither they nor I see any conflict between a sound Christian healing ministry and sound medical practice. One of the major activities of the Acorn Christian Healing Trust is to organize an annual conference at which half the delegates represent a medical discipline and the other half represent a spiritual discipline. We find we learn much from each other. The same is true of the doctor/clergy group which meets at the post-graduate medical centre of our local hospital. It is good that we should listen to each other, respect each other and pray for each other.

Healing and prayer

Our healing services include a period of general prayer usually led by the preacher. Although I like it to be extempore, it will follow certain principles. Having learned from quite a number of mistakes I believe that this is not a time to name names or to list medical conditions. Christian healing is an encounter with the living Christ, not a mulling over of ailments. So the prayers basically practise the presence of Christ, but then bring the intercessions of the people into that presence by a simple act. Hundreds of people ask for our prayers, and their names are written in an intercession book. Their needs are known in every detail to God, so we simply lift the book before God and ask that his holy and healing will be done in the lives of all whose names are in the book and also in the lives of all whose names would be there were it not for ignorance and error on our part.

We often use a 'ring of peace' method of prayer. First we set ourselves within God's peace, then we include all those people for whom we have a concern, including those whose names are in the book, and finally we imagine the ring of God's peace extending around our neighbourhood, our nation, our world and all creation. We affirm God's purpose, his power, his ultimate victory, and his eternal kingdom. We channel that which we affirm to all for whom we pray. It is a positive method of prayer. We feel not drained but refreshed by it.

The hymn of praise which ends the service follows very naturally from all that has gone before. Praise is a vital element in healing worship, and it is the element which I hope will abide in the memory of all in the congregation after a healing service.

Follow-up

The cup of coffee which follows the service is important, in that it provides a simple excuse for staying and talking. The talk can sometimes become deep and therapeutic, and though we do not encourage conversations at the moment of the laying on of hands, afterwards at coffee-time it can go on for a long time.

There may also be cause for evangelistic follow-up. A prayer of response may have been used publicly during the service; and even if it has not, some may have used it privately. I know of many who have begun or significantly deepened their Christian commitment at healing services. This is to be expected. I can think of at least three good reasons why Christian healing services are natural occasions for effective evangelism.

There is, firstly, a blend of need and expectancy characterizing the attitudes of the worshippers. Next, a good healing service is non-manipulative. The preacher will speak of human need and of the Christian resources which can meet that need, but having given a word of encouragement and a word of invitation he or she will stand back and wait. This is essential if either healing or evangelism is to take place. There can be no forceable feeding. If a response is somehow engineered, there may be a semblance of healing or a semblance of conversion but both will be false. They will melt away in the cold light of day, leaving a bitter feeling of manipulation and betrayal. However if people have discerned truth and love in Christ and have accepted it without being pressurized, then the next day truth will still be truth and the loveliness of Jesus will be lovelier than ever.

A final factor which makes a Christian healing service a natural channel of evangelism is its underpinning concept that Jesus makes a difference. The trouble with some of our other services is that they appear to be non-events. A pleasant hymn or two, a few comfortable prayers, a little nodding-off during the sermon, and a feeling that somehow duty has been done when the service is over. None of this may do any harm, but none of it is likely to shake the foundations of life. The real Jesus did not offer comfortable pleasantries to his contemporaries. He offered them a difference in outlook, in purpose, and in the fundamental nature of life. He offered not merely to give people that difference, but to *be* that difference within them. That difference is the essence of both Christian healing and evangelism. In it they are absolutely one.

5 Kingdoms in Collision: Spiritual Warfare

The sharing of good news is not only an invitation to new life in the love of God; it is an invitation to spiritual warfare. There is one particular place in Scripture which summarizes what we are trying to explore in this chapter. It is 2 Corinthians 4.4–5, where the apostle Paul writes, 'The god of this age has blinded the minds of unbelievers so they cannot see the light of the Gospel of the glory of Christ who is the image of God. For we do not preach ourselves but Jesus Christ as Lord.' Paul is in no doubt that the preaching of the gospel is a direct challenge to the rule and influence which the evil one exerts over the darkened minds of the unconverted.

Offering people salvation, then, declares war on the kingdom of Satan at the same time as challenging the unbeliever to repent. Consequently, evangelism involves both a decision to follow Jesus Christ and the deliverance of a heart and mind which is to some degree under the influence of our spiritual foe. It is no wonder that Paul describes conversion as being rescued from the dominion of darkness and brought into the kingdom of the Son (Colossians 1.13–14). We should not be surprised at how fiercely opposed the work of evangelism is, because it is one of the primary spearheads in our spiritual warfare against the Devil and his network of demonic activity. The offer and proclamation of the gospel of Christ is in effect to witness the collision of two kingdoms which are very much opposed to one another: the kingdom of God and the kingdom of darkness. This will always be so until Christ returns and fulfils once and for all the rule and reign of God in the hearts of all people.

Before we develop this subject further, there are a few factors to be borne in mind. One is the general interest in deliverance ministry within the Church, along with the dangers of focusing too much on the presence of the demonic. C.S. Lewis wrote this: 'There are two equal and opposite errors into which our race can fall about the devils. One is to disbelieve in their existence. The other is to believe, and to feel an excessive and unhealthy interest in them.'[1] For the Church, the subject of spiritual warfare is a very serioius one.

We need also to root our understanding of demonic encounter and strategy in Scripture. The Bible reveals a depth of awareness of the forces of darkness and a commitment to spiritual battle. Believers are sometimes referred to as soldiers in this warfare (Philippians 2.25). Elsewhere the apostle Paul underlines the need for spiritual authority as the proper weapons of spiritual warfare (2 Corinthians 10.4ff). The letter to the Ephesians takes it for granted that the Church knows where the real battle for souls lies: not against fallen humanity but against the powers of darkness which seek to dominate their affairs; the writer exhorts the faithful to be equipped with the necessary armour to win this war (Ephesians 6.10–18).

This biblical mandate to engage in warfare is written into our liturgy, especially the baptism service. When we baptize people into the faith of Christ according to the rites of the Church of England, the minister says, 'I sign you with the sign of the cross, the sign of Christ. Do not be ashamed to confess the faith of Christ crucified; fight valiantly under the banner of Christ against sin, the world, and the devil, and continue as his faithful soldier and

servant to the end of your life.' Baptism, therefore, is something akin to being enlisted in the army of Christ as well as
a sacrament of induction into the life of the Church.

We have already stressed that Jesus's commission to
share the good news of the kingdom of God cannot be
divided up. It contains the command to proclaim the gospel and to heal, and also to practise the ministry of deliverance. These are presented as a unified and single
commission to the whole Church of Christ. This means
that God's commission to the Church is to bring healing
not only to our physical needs but to every area of human
experience. Salvation heals our relationship with God;
reconciliation heals our relationship with each other and
with our family and community; inner healing heals our
relationship with ourselves as we learn to be set free from
the power of our own actions or the effects of other
people's actions on our lives. Very often, however, blocking our pathway to healing lie the presence and influence
of evil spirits which need to be confronted and removed in
the power and authority of Jesus. Before examining how
evangelism and spiritual warfare collide, let us clarify
what we understand by the ministry of deliverance.

Deliverance from evil

Deliverance, according to Father Jim McManus,[2] means
breaking the bondages which prevent us enjoying the
growth and healing which God has for each of us. He
gives the analogy of a cut finger. Usually we would bathe
the wound, apply some antiseptic and a plaster, and in
the morning the finger should be fine. However, if the
finger has been cut on a dirty nail and not attended to,
sooner or later it will begin to throb. Even if we then
wash the wound it will still be festering in the morning.
In other words before this wound can be properly healed
the poison must first be removed. In the spiritual life we

receive many upsets and personal wounds but if they are uninfected then it is healing that is normally needed. However, if an evil spirit has infected that wound with the poison of bondage, then deliverance is necessary before healing can take place.

Deliverance means more than being rescued from danger: it implies being taken back to God. It is not an end in itself but a necessary release which enables us to go on to grow in grace and the knowledge of Christ. The focus for deliverance then is the same as salvation and this is a clue as to how evangelism often links in with deliverance from whatever form of evil is holding us back from embracing the gospel of Christ. It also needs to be pointed out that deliverance is not just from evil spirits. We can understand this better if we briefly survey the three traditional battle zones in which the Christian is continually engaged.

THE DEVIL

The Scriptures present evil not just as the product of people's misguided choices, but also as the work of evil spirits who are busy behind the scenes. In the past there has been a tendency to dismiss both the supernatural and the demonic elements in the Bible as being the product of a worldview which has no place in modern society. However, it is now being recognized that this approach not only violates the scriptural message but also ignores a growing mass of evidence for the presence of spiritual powers. No less a historian than Jeffrey Burton Russell recognizes the centrality of cosmic–earthly spiritual warfare to salvation history.[3] The Bible does not account for the origin of Satan or evil spirits: the biblical writers are far more concerned about the fact of their existence and teaching people how to recognize them and overcome them. We need to be able to say with the apostle Paul 'we are not unaware of their schemes' (2 Corinthians 2.11).

We are not trying here to make a definitive statement as to the nature of demonic operations in the world and against the individual. On the other hand we must take this subject seriously and not be dismissive of it. We should heed the biblical warning that our spiritual battle is not really against people but against 'the powers of this dark world and against spiritual forces of evil in the heavenly realms' (Ephesians 6.12). Consequently we must learn how to confront such powers appropriately, recognize where they are at work and break the hold they have on others.

The prime focus for this confrontation is the work of evangelism. The commission which Jesus gave to his disciples contains the injunction to take authority and power to cast out evil spirits. Yet this was coupled with them being sent out to proclaim the good news of the kingdom of God. When the seventy returned from preaching they revealed that even the demons were subject to them in the name of Christ (Luke 10.17ff). Jesus immediately declared that their gospel witness was in effect the dismantling of Satan's influence. But he drew their attention away from that victory over evil spirits to the fact that they had received the good news and consequently that their names were written in the book of life.

If we take seriously our church's witness to the community and wish to bring people into a healing relationship with God and others, then somewhere along this road we will encounter the powers of evil who will resist our work. Let us take our power and authority over evil seriously and learn how to be spiritually prepared to fight and how to handle our weapons of warfare.

THE WORLD

The apostle John exhorts us to 'love not the world neither the things that are in the world . . . for all that is in the world, the lust of the flesh, and the lust of the eyes, and the pride of life, is not of the Father but of the world' (1 John 2.15–16). Here the world is not that of nature and creation but is rather understood as those ideas and practices which reflect fallen humanity. John's words are not a command to retreat from the world and become a hermit but rather to live in the world according to Christian values and where necessary to oppose and refuse to live by a fallen world's so-called standards. This is graphically stated in J.B. Phillips' paraphrase of Romans 12.1–2 which says, 'Don't let the world around you squeeze you into its own mould, but let God re-mould your minds from within, so that you may prove in practice that the plan of God for you is good, meets all his demands and moves towards the goal of true maturity.'[4]

For some years I worked in industry and in particular in oil refineries where I worked with a team of men applying safety film to windows. Very often we worked abroad and were given a certain amount of money to cover our food and accommodation but we were expected to return any money left over. A number of the men would overstate their expenses and return only a little money, keeping the rest for themselves. The Christians on the team felt that this was dishonest and refused to go along with this practice. This immediately created friction among us. For the duration of the work trip there would be a continuous verbal battle aimed at those who would not go along with the majority and pretend that they had spent more money than they actually had. It felt oppressive and painful to say the least. As Christians we wished to avoid greed and dishonesty and yet disliked intensely the confrontation that resulted, even though we had no intention of informing on those who were dishonest. The temptation was to take the easy way out and go along with everybody else in order to keep the peace. In other words we needed deliverance from the temptation to compromise. While this was not deliverance from an evil spirit within a life in the classic possession state, it was just as much a part of the spiritual warfare that Christians and the Church are called to fight.

Although the Bible speaks of the world as being under the power of Satan who is called the god of this world (2 Corinthians 4.4), very often the kind of warfare required focuses more on the results of Satan's influence than on any direct conflict with evil spirits. We must not forget that the Church is in conflict with some of the attitudes, beliefs and lifestyles of the world in which it lives and to which it is called to be a witness. This is the constant tension involved in being a servant to the community, as well as the challenge.

The Church of Christ is commissioned to fight on the frontiers of justice and peace, to uphold standards of honesty and integrity in personal and business relationships, to campaign for better living conditions for the poor, for increased commitment to the Third World, for equality for women and for an end to racial prejudice and corruption, to name but a few. This will undoubtedly bring us into conflict with the vested interests of business conglomerates on the one hand and the convictions of individuals on the other. At times the Church has fallen prey to the same sins as the world around it, and it needs to be released from these in order to regain its authority as a witness. This is what lies behind the challenge of the glorified Jesus to some of the churches mentioned in the Book of Revelation. The churches of Pergamum and Thyatira were commanded to repent because they had adopted the sexual practices of the community in which they lived and not the way of holiness (Revelation 2.12–29).

Refusal to repent and be delivered from evil implies the loss of power to evangelize. So part of the spiritual battle is against the world where the Church is to maintain God's standards for itself and to seek opportunities to plant such godly ways of living as it can within a fallen society. If the Church has failed it needs to recognize where it has fallen and repent and be delivered from the sins of its society.

The Church, like the leaders of the people of Israel in the Old Testament, is also called to confess the sins of the community in which it lives, and to pray that God would set individuals and nations free from their sins. Examples of this form of warfare prayer can be seen in the lives of Daniel and Ezra who though not guilty of the sins of their community, nevertheless come before God and pray 'O Lord, we have sinned.'

THE FLESH

This is the term used in the New Testament to describe in the main a life which is self-centred rather than God-centred. Ray Steadman defines the flesh as 'that proud ego, that uncrucified self which is the seat of wilful disobedience and rebellion against authority'.[5] Unlike the warfare concerning the world which is community-based, war against the flesh represents the struggle on a personal level whereby our flawed humanity is inclined towards self-centredness, involving our minds, emotions and will. Perhaps the most important book in the Bible about the sad affairs of the flesh is that of Galatians where the term is used seventeen times. Here Paul contrasts lives lived in the flesh and those lived in the Spirit where he describes the activities of the flesh (or 'sinful nature' in the New International Version) and the fruit of the Spirit. The activities of the flesh include sexual immorality, spiritual deviancy such as witchcraft and idolatry, emotions of hatred ranging from discord to jealousy and rage, selfish ambitions and destructive behaviour such as drunkeness and orgies. The fruits of the Spirit, on the other hand, which we are to grow in our hearts, are love and joy, peace and patience, kindness and goodness, faithfulness, gentleness and self-control

(Galatians 5.19–21). Paul goes on to say that the Christian life is one where we daily put to death the activities of the sinful nature and walk in the Spirit of Christ. This battlefield is within us and is constantly to be fought and is managed on a number of levels.

Temptation

We are all subject to temptation as Jesus was himself, and this is demonstrated by his trials in the wilderness. In Genesis 3, the temptation of Adam and Eve has three strands: God's word (3.1), self-deception (3.4), and disobedience (3.5). As a result temptation, by appealing to our desires, provokes us to sinful activity which separates us from God and brings condemnation.

Part of our spiritual warfare is the struggle to resist temptation like Jesus did, to be obedient to God's word and rely on the power of the Holy Spirit to help us overcome. When we do give in to temptations we will need to be restored in our walk with God. This is why Jesus included in the prayer he taught us 'deliver us from evil'. This is at the heart of evangelism, that we might be forgiven and set free from living a sinful life. Sometimes this can be a struggle because sin is addictive and often we have to go through a withdrawal period as we endeavour to live another way thanks to the grace of God. It is at this precise point that prayers of deliverance from the habit of sinning are needed. Being tempted does not mean that there has to be something wrong with us, as the example of Jesus illustrates. I always remember a lecturer telling us, 'sin is nice!' He went on to say that sin is attractive, which is why we do it so often; and unless it appeals to us in some way temptation is not temptation.

Accusation

Some years ago I was praying with a minister who was on the verge of giving up his work as a pastor and looking for some other kind of work. He was quite depressed and upset at his situation. He told me that he had recently had a serious argument with one of his church members who had pointed out to him all his mistakes and told him that he was no good at his job. 'I always feel a failure,' he told me, 'and when Jack told me what he felt about my ministry it just felt too much to carry on.' As I listened to his story he revealed that he had battled for years with feelings of inadequacy and fraudulancy and he had come to the end of his tether. These feelings reached back into his childhood when his father was always pointing out his mistakes and telling him that he would never amount to much. As a result his self-worth was greatly diminished and his sense of the love and work of God in his life was greatly overshadowed. This man needed deliverance from the power of the 'accuser' in his life, from the relentless message that he was a failure. In his case deliverance took the form of recognizing the truth of God's love and owning it more deeply; in the light of this he was able to renounce the accusation heaped against him. He felt encouraged and empowered to continue with his life and ministry renewed in the Holy Spirit.

One of the titles used in the Bible of Satan is 'accuser' (thirty-four times). On the whole the term refers to the act of bringing a verbal judgement against another. An example of this is in Revelation 12–10, where Satan is depicted as a prosecutor in the courts of heaven where he brings charges against the people of God (cf. Job 1.9–11). What this means is that our spiritual enemy seizes on half-truths and innuendo and uses them to assault our hearts and minds. It is not only our total failures which are weapons at his disposal but also our lesser imperfections and faults, and the awareness of our many weaknesses. We are reminded of all these and led to feel unworthy of God's service or blessing and consequently come to a halt in our Christian lives. We need to be delivered from these accusations by focusing once again on the love and grace of God, to repent of having doubted God's care of us.

Spiritual strongholds

Paul exhorts his readers to give the devil no 'foothold' in their lives (Ephesians 4.27). The Greek word means a special place or sanctuary, referring to any area in our lives which has not been yielded to the Holy Spirit for healing or cleansing. In Ephesians Paul has been writing about persistent sinning or a long-term breakdown in the fellowship of the church. Such a lack of discipline has the effect of giving a special place or influence to the powers of evil, and this needs to be rooted out of our lives if our faith and love are not to be compromised. Just repentance may not be enough; we may need to pray with authority that the hold which we have given to the evil spirits be broken and their effects removed from our lives and our churches. The hallmark of true renewal and revival has often been when cleansing and deliverance from evil first begins in the Church.

Perhaps an extension of this type of warfare is the area of personal strongholds. Paul uses very powerful imagery when he talks of setting us free from evil and speaks about 'demolishing strongholds' (2 Corinthians 10.3–6). Tom White defines a stronghold as 'an entrenched pattern of thought, an ideology, value or behaviour that is contrary to the word and will of God'.[6] An example of this kind of stronghold is the story of Ann, who grew up in a family where she was repeatedly and harshly criticized and told how bad she was and how much of a failure she would always be. Although she had become a Christian, no matter how hard she tried to think otherwise she had persistent conviction that she was a failure and that God might well love and bless everybody else, but not her. Such a conviction did not diminish even after counselling and prayer ministry. Eventually she recognized that, owing to her painful upbringing, she had inadvertently given room to Satan who used this unhealed wound to exercise a hold over her life. She only improved when she recognized the need for a level of deliverance and received this ministry. Now she was able to overcome her crippling debility and progress in her faith and life.

This certainly coheres with what Paul writes because he describes three kinds of strongholds: arguments, pretensions and memories. These can all become areas through which evil spirits seek to gain access to our inner life and exert a level of influence and control. Often, therefore, before we can deal with the issue in question, we may first have to break the hold of an evil spirit so that the individual is freed to work through the changes which God requires in their lives. Occasionally this may require the help of someone with more experience in deliverance because there is a greater degree of demonic influence. This brings us to the subject of what we understand by possession.

Possession by evil

When I was addressing this subject at a meeting I asked those present which story from the Bible immediately came to their mind when it was said that someone was demon possessed. By far the majority present said that it was the story of Legion with its frightening picture of extreme demonic infestation. Clearly, though, the Legion scenario is not the predominant model of possession within the New Testament and it presents an unusually severe form of demonization. Jesus delivered the daughter of the Syro-Phoenician woman without even going to see her (Matthew 15.21–8); he tells Peter that

Satan was to sift him like wheat but the way of escape would come through intercessory prayer (Luke 22.31); and other forms of deliverance are by a straightforward command without any outward manifestation at all. The word used in the New Testament is 'daimonidsomai' and is more accurately translated as 'having a spirit' or 'being bothered by a spirit'. This suggests a range of demonic influence rather than the extreme picture presented by the usual translation of 'demon possession'. I personally do not believe that a committed Christian would be of the Legion status because he or she has the help of the indwelling presence of the Holy Spirit.

Praying for deliverance

Let us conclude this section with some cautionary words. We need to recognize that deliverance is not just being set free from evil spirits but also from the consequences of living in a fallen world, and all the wrong choices and habits we have acquired in our lives. This is why it is so important to discern the actual nature of a person's distress before praying the deliverance prayer. Jim McManus suggests that one way of doing this is to pray silently and command any evil power over a person's life to be broken and removed and then pray audibly for whatever healing concern they bring. He reports that many people are freed from their bonds in this way and it also serves as a precaution in case our discernment is mistaken. I think that this is admirable advice except for those instances of more severe spiritual bondage, when the co-operation the person concerned is needed to confront the powers of evil.

It may be a good idea to pray a prayer of deliverance without introducing the subject of evil spirits. I find it very helpful to use the passage in John's epistle which says that 'if we confess our sins, he [Jesus] is faithful and just and will forgive us our sins and purify us from all unrighteousness' (1 John 1.9). The unrighteousness is all the harmful consequences the person has been struggling with which have caused them hurt. I use all the language of a deliverance prayer which involves binding and commanding to leave. Sometimes there is a marked response in the person for whom I am praying and at other times there is a sense of gentle release. Where there is a definite response I usually stop the prayer and discuss with the person what is happening and then together we take a step of faith and continue the prayer but this time commanding any bondage caused by an evil spirit to be broken and the person to be set free. Then I proceed with prayers for healing and renewal.

It is always advisable to consult others more experienced before engaging in any form of deliverance prayer; apart from being a wise precaution, it helps you recognize the nature of a person's distress. Most Anglican dioceses have a deliverance advisory team and your minister would be able to contact them for advice and assistance.

Spiritual warfare and evangelism

Why does evangelism engage us in spiritual warfare and the ministry of deliverance? It is immediately apparent that the sharing of the gospel, however it is done, is a call, a challenge and a commitment. Because Jesus invites us to come and follow him, it is a call to discipleship in which we embrace his lordship of our lives. That is why we can command the powers of darkness to submit to Jesus, because we have done it ourselves and have come under his power and authority.

Evangelism is not just an appeal to live a better life; it is a challenge to recognize who Jesus is. It is a summons to recognize the claims of God as our creator and sustainer as well as a challenge to the Church to be witnesses to these things. Evangelism is a commitment to live lives lit with Christ-like love and power in a world which is in spiritual darkness. Christians are called, challenged and committed to seeing the kingdom of God established in our communities. So to engage in evangelism is to live on the frontier where the kingdom of God clashes with the kingdom of darkness in a struggle that will not be over until Christ himself returns to establish his kingdom on earth.

THE CHRIST WHO CONQUERS

The conflict between the two kingdoms is seen above all at the cross. It was not just a good man who died there for us but the sinless Son of God. The death of Jesus Christ makes forgiveness and salvation possible. The fact of his coming into the world and going to Calvary was a declaration that the king had come into his own country and was freeing all those enslaved to the rule of Satan. Paul combines these themes when he writes that the work of Christ on the cross was to offer freedom as well as to disarm the spiritual powers which hold humankind in slavery: 'Having disarmed the powers and authorities, he made a public spectacle of them, triumphing over them by the cross' (Colossians 2.15). The cross is where spiritual warfare is successfully conducted. The cross is Christ's demonstration that the rule of Satan is broken and it represents God's initiative in taking spiritual warfare into the enemy's territory.

THE KINGDOM WHICH IS COMING

Jesus taught his disciples that evangelism proclaims by word and deed, in healing and deliverance, that the kingdom of God has come. In other words, evangelism was a kingdom initiative in which the work of dismantling the structures of evil within each life would begin. The apostle Paul described the conversion of the Colossian Christians as being delivered out of the dominion of darkness and brought into the kingdom of the Son (Colossians 1.13). In the same way, when a parish church holds a mission or shares the gospel within its neighbourhood, it is part of the advance of God's kingdom into the kingdom of darkness. Knowing this, we should be faithful in praying for our pastors and those involved in evangelism, that they and their families may be protected and that they may with authority engage in spiritual warfare. Evangelism more than any sign or wonder, work or power, reminds the forces of darkness that their influence among people is being eroded and that it signals their complete defeat when Jesus returns.

THE CALL TO CHANGE

Salvation is a call to holiness and the beginning of a personal pilgrimage to become more like Christ in character and conduct. Consequently, every type of evil influence in a person's life which opposes this process needs to be removed. Holiness is not a cosmetic luxury to make our Christian lives more appealing; it is a difficult path to tread, but one by which sin's inroads to our hearts are healed and we are restored to a fuller humanity. It means calling on all our resources of faith to confront our many weaknesses if we are to keep going until the end of the journey.

THE CHALLENGE OF COMMUNITY

The work of salvation is not an isolated experience to be kept to ourselves or contained within the fellowship of the church. It is the making of community. In the Old Testament we find the model of the nation which serves God and this is its witness to the countries around it. In the New Testament there is the model of the Church which is the new Israel. Evangelicals have been very conscientious in challenging the individual to repentance and new life in Jesus Christ; but we must also have the vision of new life in the city and town and parish. The work of evangelism creates the community of the Church which then shares its experience with its society in order to extend the godly community to the city. However, in seeking to do this we encounter the powers of evil which are part of the web of community life. Part of the gospel strategy must therefore be to discern the ills of that community and confront them with the message of healing and evangelism. The Church in fact has the commission both to celebrate and confess on behalf of its community. There is the encouragement to pray for the peace of the city in Psalm 122.6 and there is the example of Jesus weeping over the city which turns away from the good news (Matthew 23.37).

Jesus said that there was more rejoicing among the angels over one sinner who repents than over a host of others who do not need to repent (Luke 15.7,9). Every experience of salvation is one more signal of the coming fulfilment of the kingdom of God and the impending end of the rule of Satan (see, for example, Revelation 12).

I am quite sure that it is no coincidence that the Decade of Evangelism has also seen an increased awareness and involvement in spiritual warfare and the work of deliverance. Evangelism is not a comfortable work: it disturbs the very fabric of evil influence within individuals and community in a comprehensive way. As we engage in mission we should be committed both to prayer and to learning about spiritual warfare. Then our witness will be more effective, and we shall see more and more people being changed within the community.

6 Evangelism and Healing in Bereavement Care

It sometimes seems to me that evangelism is not unlike jujitsu! Jujitsu is a Japanese word with the surprising meaning of 'gentleness', because although it is a martial art it is non-aggressive. Its plan of campaign always involves *response to somebody else's movements*. My dictionary says it is an 'art of self defence without weapons that depends for its efficiency largely upon the principle of making use of an opponent's strength and weight'. Your opponent's energy is incorporated into your efforts.

It makes a lot of sense to apply a similar principle to the spread of the gospel: to be aware of things that are happening around us and moves that are being made towards us, to work them into our strategy of evangelism, rather than wasting energy by initiating completely new procedures. In other words it is easier to *take* opportunites than to *make* them. The same thing applies to the healing ministry. It makes sense not to go out and search for needs and opportunities without making sure that we have dealt with the needs and opportunities for ministry which come to us of their own accord.

This chapter and the next will deal with three occasions when people who rarely darken the door of a Christian church change their habits and actually beat their way to the church's door with some determination. It happens when there is a baby to be baptized, a marriage to be solemnized or a funeral service to be conducted.

It is an open secret that not all clergy take these approaches as seriously as they might. We talk rather flippantly about 'the hatched, matched and despatched' or 'the four-wheelers' who come to church first in a pram, then in a taxi and finally in a hearse. But it is my strong feeling that if we give less than our best to baptisms, weddings and funerals a major opportunity for evangelism and healing is missed. Let us take them in reverse order and in this chapter look first at funerals and at caring for the bereaved.

When I was a theological student I found myself at the receiving end of many hours of lectures on the niceties of academic theology. We wrestled with the names and theories of wide range of international scholars. In contrast there was just one forty-five-minute talk about how to take a funeral. It was hardly a balanced use of time. When I became a curate, academic theology was little in demand, but I spent hour after hour in matters related to the conduct of funerals. My personal record was taking seventeen funerals in one week! I had to work out the principles of bereavement care as best I could. My overworked vicar gave such help as he could but I had to learn by experience and in some cases by horrendous mistakes.

Funeral services on their own, though, do not provide adequate bereavement care, however sensitively they may be conducted, and the clergy on their own do not have time to offer the hours of pastoral care which are needed before and after a funeral. Effective bereavement care requires a team in which clergy and laity work together.

This is how it has worked out in my present parish of Prenton. It is a scheme which was initiated by a hospital sister and developed by the wife of one of our curates; it is now headed up by a member of our congregation who before his retirement supervised the churches' counselling service on Merseyside. The sequence of ministry goes like this.

The telephone rings at the vicarage and a local under-taker tells the parish secretary about a death. If some-one in the congregation has died, we will probably know already; if not, we will need to know the name and address and age of the deceased person, details of the next of kin, the date of death and if possible the cause, and as many other details as are available. The time and place and style of the funeral service will be arranged. We will quickly decide which of the clergy will be taking the service. We usually make a prelimin-ary visit so that the family can feel they know us and so that we can find out as much as possible about the person who has died and about the people to whom we will be ministering.

Before we come away we leave behind us the first of the parish leaflets which we have produced as an aid to bereavement support. It begins: 'This leaflet comes to you with the sympathy and love of the congregations of St Stephen's and St Alban's, Prenton. Please contact us at any time using the telephone number at the foot of the next page'. It goes on to set out briefly the hope offered by the Christian faith in the face of sorrow and bereave-ment, and asks the family to pray for the funeral service itself. It ends by promising that the church will keep in touch with the bereaved and assures them of our love and prayers.

The leaflet also contains a list of helpful telephone numbers – the Samaritans, the DSS (who publish the leaflet 'What to do after a death'), the Citizen's Advice Bureau, Age Concern, the nearest Cruse club, and of course the number of our vicarage and parish office, so that the family can easily make contact again before the funeral.

On the day of the funeral we try to see that the ser-vice embodies certain principles. First of all we speak simply about the aims of the funeral and assure the congregation not only that they will have time and opportunity to make their own personal act of commemoration, respect and thanksgiving within the privacy of their own minds but that we will help them to do so within the framework of the Christian faith and of the healing which it can bring. We speak simply of our conviction that there is life after death and that if we place our trust in Jesus we can face the prospect of eternity not fearfully but in the hope and expectation that the best is yet to be. We offer a gentle but specific challenge to all the mourners to reflect on the pattern of their life and the state of their soul, and as the service ends we give the chief mourner a card containing appropriate prayers and Bible passages.

Usually family and friends will keep a close eye on the chief mourner for a week or so after the funeral, but a fortnight after the service when this care and attention may be diminishing, a letter will be sent out by our parish office. This assures them that the church has not forgotten them and asks whether one of the congregation may call in a few weeks time to see how things are going and to offer any practical help that may be needed. One of two prayers is enclosed. The first, called 'A prayer for the one who is left', has proved a healing prayer in cases of deep grief, as in the loss of a husband or wife. The second, the prayer of St Francis of Assisi ('Lord make us instruments of thy peace'), is suitable when the grief is less deep.

We allow a few days to pass and then if we have not received a phone call or letter to say that a visit would be unwelcome, we notify our bereavement support team about the details they will need to know so that the parish ministry can continue through their care.

Whoever has taken the funeral will have filled in a form providing details about the life and death of the deceased person along with information about the next of kin and their family. Equipped with this the visitor will call round. He or she will take a further pamphlet which we have compiled to help mourners deal with the continuing experience of bereavement. This identifies a number of milestones which characterize the life of those who mourn: disbelief, mental confusion, exhaustion, guilt and anger, rejection and grief, followed by a return to reality and acceptance. The typical feelings at each stage of the recovery process are briefly described, for example:

- You often feel unreasonably tired and use up reserves of energy in just coping. Sometimes you experience fear when doing things that have never bothered you in the past.
- Bereavement is often accompanied by a sense of guilt or regret concerning the past or by anger towards those you feel have failed you or your loved one. These feelings may not be reasonable, but this does not prevent them from being strong.

The pamphlet also suggests various signposts which may point the way to healing:

- Try to tackle problems as they arise.
- Don't be afraid of spoiling yourself just a little.
- Endeavour to cope with one day at a time.
- Try not to rush into quick decisions. Moving house and other big decisions should not be tackled too soon.
- Look for ways of helping others. That way you will begin to feel wanted and needed again.
- Remind yourself of all the things that have not changed. Many of your former pleasures are still there waiting for you.
- Look after your health and appearance and aim at a good diet.

- Sleeplessness may be a problem – a hot bath and milk drink will help. Avoid habit-forming remedies in the long term.
- New interests may help e.g. evening classes and hobbies.
- Remember that you can pray anywhere and at any time.

The visitor will offer friendship, support and basic information about the resources for healing which are available in the life of the church. If necessary several visits may be made, and on occasion the visits continue for many months.

There may or may not be a specific response to the Christian gospel on the part of those who are visited, but they will certainly know that the clergy and people of the church really care about them, that they need never be alone, and that it is the Christian claim that Jesus will make a difference to both life and death if we give him the opportunity.

I have just been visiting Joseph. His wife died two years ago and I was invited to take the funeral. He had a caring family but they lived a long way away. Of his children and stepchildren the nearest was in London and others were scattered around the world. Soon after the funeral, our parish visitor called at his home and Joseph decided he would start coming to church. He says it was initially to say thank you for the assurance he felt that his wife, who was a firm believer, had been received into heaven, but he is still a regular member of our congregation because he says he meets 'such nice people in church'. In the absence of his own family, we are a substitute family down the road. He feels we care – and we do.

There is no guarantee that people who receive bereavement ministry and support will react in this way. What we do guarantee is that when we first contact them they will receive a hundred per cent of our attention, that at the funeral service they will hear the gospel expressed as clearly and sensitively as is in our power, and that after the funeral is over they will have the offer of loving care for as long as they wish to receive it. The visitor will be available by phone and, if given the opportunity, the congregation will be ready to welcome them in the name of Jesus.

There is perhaps one other occasion in the life of our parish which deserves a mention, because it brings together our ministries of evangelism, of healing and of care for the bereaved. It is the annual All Souls Day Communion Service.

Three or four weeks before All Souls Day, the parish office sends out a letter in the name of all the clergy who have conducted funeral services during the previous year. It is addressed to every person who has been named as next of kin, providing they live within reach of our parish, and invites them to an evening service of Holy Communion (both the confirmed and the unconfirmed). They are also invited to let us know if they want someone to be commemorated by name. We also leave sheets of paper at the back of both our churches so that members can add the names of their own friends and loved ones who have died. In due course these combine with the letters to provide us with a list of more than a hundred people.

At the All Souls service, our daughter church is usually comfortably full and normally half the congregation consists of non-churchgoers. One of our staff will speak simply about why we believe in Jesus and why it is our conviction that those who put their trust in Jesus can face both life and death without fear. Then slowly and carefully we read the list of names we have been given, commemorating each one in the presence of the God who created and loves us all. It might be a lengthy procedure but you could hear a pin drop.

We invite all those present to make their own act of Christian trust and commitment and encourage those who are not able to receive communion to receive a personal blessing instead. We sing well-known hymns and end the service on a note of praise. Afterwards there are endless cups of coffee and opportunities for all who wish to talk to do so for as long as they wish.

Perhaps it is worth reiterating that at no point during this service or during individual funeral services or during pastoral visits, do we ever manipulate bereaved people into an emotional response. There is absolutely no place in Christian evangelism or Christian healing for exploiting human needs by psychological pressure. Wherever there is need, it should be the work of the Church to seek to meet it and there can be few needs which are deeper or more agonizing than those experienced by the bereaved.

Virtually everybody undergoes the trauma of bereavement. If we claim that Jesus makes a saving and healing difference to the whole of life, then those who are experiencing the hurts and stresses of bereavement and come to us for help have a right to expect the Christian churches to put our time and our love where our mouths are. If this chapter does not provide a model for your church, I believe it is important that you find your own.

At this moment, as you read this, thousands of bereaved people, whose hearts are full of pain, are waiting for the churches' ministry and wondering whether we have any healing to offer them. Please God they may not wait in vain.

7 Weddings and Christenings: Opportunity Knocks

The clergy do not have to seek out opportunities for weddings and baptisms. They come without prompting. There is a natural flow and no priming of the pump is necessary. As with funerals they provide an opportunity for meeting needs and for offering gospel ministry, but although they offer a major opportunity to the churches it is far from easy to make the most of them. Those who come for weddings and baptisms are usually much less open to ministry in depth than those who have been bereaved.

In fact people's perception of their own need may be horrendously inadequate. Only a few days before I wrote this, I heard what may well turn out to be my matrimonial quote of the year. It came from a young bride-to-be who was determined to have a church wedding. She had arranged to wear a gorgeously extravagant wedding dress and in her own words, 'A dress like this deserves a church wedding!' It is a real temptation for the clergy to tell such folk just what they can do with their dress and their wedding. They seem to insult God and to debase the whole concept of marriage. However the temptation must be resisted.

People who come to the churches to be married have real deep needs even if initially they are unaware of many of them. There are, after all, such possibilities for good and ill in marriages. It reminds me of the nursery rhyme:

> There was a little girl who had a little curl
> Right in the middle of her forehead
> When she was good she was very very good
> But when she was bad she was horrid!

So with marriage: when it is good it is very very good –
but when it is bad – phew!

On the one hand, marriage provides a marvellous opportunity for joy and fulfilment. Speaking personally,
next to my relationship with the Lord himself, my relationship with my wife, Eira, is without doubt the most
important element in my life. I owe an eternal debt to
her. Without her life would be diminished and impover-
ished and I would be a shadow of myself. Marriage can
be a treasure hunt in which we discover each other, discover ourselves and discover God.

By contrast it can also be hell! There are so many ways in
which it can go wrong that it can end up more like a
torture chamber than a treasure hunt. It can benefit nobody
– except perhaps the lawyers who preside over the 50 per
cent of marriages which these days end in divorce or separation. Husbands and wives are hurt, children are hurt,
families and friends are hurt. Society as a whole is hurt.

With such contrasting possibilities in prospect, such
prizes and such perils, we dare not turn couples away
when they come along to a church and ask to be married. We must offer them our best ministry, the Lord's
best ministry. In order to do that we must put a great
deal of thought into working out how we may best meet
them at their point of need – a need which they may well
only dimly perceive. So once again I am going to set out
the details of what we do in Prenton, not as model but as
a starting point, a stimulus to thought and action.

When the vicarage phone rings and a voice enquires
about arranging a wedding (the unpromising phrase
which is sometimes used is 'we want to book the church

for a wedding'), I ask the couple to come round for our initial meeting. This is basically a getting-to-know-you occasion combined with a fact-finding exercise. I have to make sure I know the details which will ultimately appear on the wedding certificate – their names and addresses (or joint address if, as increasingly happens, they are living together), their occupations or professions, the names and occupations of their fathers, the proposed date of their wedding and their ages on that date. We also talk in general terms about their reason for wanting a church wedding and their ideas about marriage.

I will try to communicate the fact that marriage presents the possibility of high risks and high rewards and that it is worthwhile undertaking very careful preparation. As an immediate example of marriage preparation I offer the couple two copies of an 'expectation check-sheet'.

When marriages fail it is probably because expectations have not been met and so it makes a great deal of sense for would-be brides and grooms to find out their own expectations and those of their partner and to check their compatibility. The check-sheet we use is based on one which I was shown by a marriage counsellor some time ago and I hope its anonymous author will forgive me for both using it and adapting it.

Pre-marriage preparation: expectation check

HOW TO USE THIS LIST

(a) On your own
Tick any of these items which you personally expect to be true in your marriage.

(b) Together
Compare your expectations. (Put a cross beside your partner's expectations.) If there are differences, consider

how important they are. How are you going to resolve them?

(c) At your pre-wedding interview
There will be an opportunity to talk further about this, if you wish to do so.

REMEMBER – If marriages go wrong, it is usually because expectations and reality do not match and the couple do not know how to deal with the situation. So this is an important exercise.

WHEN WE ARE MARRIED

I expect . . .
1. The housework to be equally shared.
2. To have a joint bank account.
3. The husband will make the final decisions.
4. I will keep my old friends.
5. To have a night out weekly without my partner.
6. To lose my privacy.
7. I will miss my family.
8. We will see our in-laws once a week.
9. A meal ready for me every night.
10. To give up some of my hobbies.
11. To cut down on my social life.
12. A token of love now and again.
13. Married life will be just the same for me as it was for my parents.
14. We will make love whenever we like.
15. We will have a baby one day.
16. It will be christened in my church.
17. There will be just one wage when the family starts.
18. A long healthy life.
19. To be tempted to be unfaithful.
20. We will be together till death.
21. I will be able to change my partner's ways.

22. One of our parents will come to live with us eventually.
23. A holiday away every year.
24. A lot of hard work.
25. A lot of happiness.
26. I will change to please my partner.
27. I will give up some of my favourite foods.
28. When my partner *really* knows me, I will still be loved.
29. We will take the Christian faith seriously together.
30. Being Christians will make a difference to our marriage.

As the expectation check-sheets are given to wedding couples, they are also invited to take part in a course of four marriage preparation sessions. These are conducted not by the clergy but by two members of the congregation, who have developed special skills in this sphere. The sessions deal with social, psychological, sexual and spiritual aspects of marriage and are not so much periods of teaching as times of discovery.

For a start each is asked the following questions. How well (or badly) do you think you know your partner? Does he/she take sugar in coffee? What colour are his/her eyes? How many children does he/she want? Is he/she ambitious? Does he/she enjoy his/her work? What newspaper does he/she read? How does he/she vote? Did he/she have a happy childhood? Is he/she tidy or untidy? How much does he/she earn? What time does he/she like to go to bed? Does he/she like cooking? Does he/she like an early cup of tea? What is his/her favourite place? What does he/she like to do on holiday? What time of the day is he/she at his/her best? What makes him/her angry or annoyed? What treat does he/she like best? Does he/she like children? How does he/she like to relax?

Questions like these serve as a basis for each to listen to and understand the other more deeply. They also enable each to see himself or herself through the other's eyes. By the time refreshments come along at the end of the session, they may well be needed!

In the second session couples are asked to look again at expectations and roles and particularly to consider how to deal with times of conflict. Will they recognize and acknowledge areas of conflict or try to pretend conflict does not exist? If conflict is recognized, will each be willing and ready to look at the other's point of view and to identify underlying causes and needs, even though this may be painful? Will there be a willingness to listen, to learn, to accept responsibility, to say sorry, and to change? Couples are asked to make a list of topics or situations which most commonly trigger off disagreements and cause rows. They are also asked to think of an argument which has had a happy conclusion and to work out the good and positive things which were learned, which can be used as ground rules in the future.

This is a natural context in which to talk about in-law problems and about budgeting and the right use of money. It is also a good time to clarify hopes, expectations and fears about having children and to discuss the effect of children on marriage.

The third session is about growing together sexually. While realizing that many couples have intercourse before marriage and some live together, this session will in no way apologize for basic Christian convictions or sell them short.

Our sexuality is God's good gift, important and meant to be enjoyed, but it is also hazardous and may be affected by many things in society and in our own past – childhood experiences, family attitudes, good and bad relationships, myths and misinformation and possibly trauma from abuse. It is better to talk about these things than not to talk, though much of that will probably take place privately after the session has finished.

It is useful to have suitable visual aids for this session – diagrams, videos, etc. – both to provide information (because many couples do not know nearly as much as they think they do!) and also to stimulate thought and discussion. We also find that this is a natural point to introduce the biblical concepts of 'one flesh' and the importance of 'leaving and cleaving'. It is a good time to begin to consider the meaning of the wedding service.

The fourth session is about growing together emotionally and spiritually. Couples are asked these questions: 'Do you both have the same convictions about God? Do you ever talk to each other about him? Was there a time in your life when God has felt particularly close to you? Why do you want to make your wedding vows before God and have his blessing on your marriage?' They are also asked 'What do you mean by love? Is it just a feeling of romance or is it more than that? Can you still love when you are angry, resentful, hurt, tired and depressed? How far is love an act of commitment and of will? What is meant by the words "I will" in the marriage service?'

Couples are invited to look in detail at the marriage vows they will be making in the service. Does the bride wish the word 'obey' to be included or omitted in her vows? Will they both mean what they say? Where will they look for help in days of difficulty? What is distinctive and special about *Christian* marriage? Couples are invited to select a reading or a prayer for their own service and to say why it is significant for them, and this leads naturally to ending the fourth session with a time of prayer.

A fortnight before the wedding there is a final meeting at the vicarage so that I can check all the information once again and we can go through the details of the service. In the case of those couples who have not attended the preparation course (which is not obligatory though it is strongly recommended) I add a short summary of some of its main ingredients.

Finally the day of the wedding service arrives. We try to conduct each service as though it were the only wedding ever to be conducted in our church. We challenge the congregation to be more than spectators, to follow the whole service with their thoughts and prayers so that together we can lay a true foundation for the marriage we are witnessing and affirming. We invite all those who are married to quietly reaffirm their own marriage vows as the bride and groom make theirs. We offer a special welcome to non-churchgoers and invite them to spend a few quiet moments with God, asking him for any guidance or help which may be appropriate in their lives. Our hope is that the service will be meaningful and memorable at many levels not just for the bride and groom but to all who are present.

We make clear to the bride and groom that our interest in them will not cease as the marriage service comes to an end, but that we offer an 'after-sales service' and that they will always be welcome if they want to come back for discussion or advice at any time in the future. Then once a year they are invited back to a service of reaffirmation of marriage vows at a mid-summer evening service.

It is my conviction that this sequence of marriage preparation and support can be an important channel for evangelism and healing. Of course different couples react in very different ways. Some welcome every opportunity and use all our facilities to the full. Others show little interest and though they may be spending hours arranging and preparing the trimmings of the marriage – the wedding dress, the flowers, the photos, the reception – they seem to feel it is quite unnecessary to prepare for marriage itself.

A fair number of our marriage couples, however, give us the opportunity for further ministry when they return in due course to arrange a christening. I am aware that throughout the Church as a whole there are different baptismal policies. At one extreme there is the 'hard line' which denies baptism to all except the families of regular churchgoers and committed Christians. At the other extreme there is the 'soft touch' which provides christenings for all comers with no questions asked. Between the extremes there are various intermediate positions. My own concern here is not to argue for any particular policy but to suggest that wherever we may find ourselves in the baptismal spectrum it is important that we should see the therapeutic and evangelistic potential of the opportunities which baptisms bring to us.

In Prenton all our baptisms are outreach services. We hold them at the monthly family services which take place at both our churches. There may be over a hundred in the baptismal parties alone and most of these will usually be non-churchgoers. Here is a major opportunity to communicate what it means to accept the Christian faith and belong to the Christian Church.

Let me try to give a picture of a typical family service. As the congregation come in, one of our guitar groups will be playing and singing, creating a friendly atmosphere. After an informal welcome and a short summary of parish notices and news, we check that all the babies we are expecting are present. We point out that mums and dads can take toddlers to the children's corner at any point in the service if it is helpful and that they will find plenty of books, cuddly toys and other playthings there.

Then we begin the service with a well-known traditional hymn led by the organ and choir as the uniformed organizations bring up their flags and banners. This is followed by an opening prayer in which we approach

God together and ask his blessing on our worship. Then, after further singing led by the group, we present our teaching spot. This is likely to be a presentation with visual aids and including lots of participation by the congregation and especially by the children. It always leads into an explanation of some aspect of baptism.

For instance one Sunday we had hidden a dozen chocolate bars and a dozen little candles around the church and all the children present were encouraged to take part in a treasure hunt, helped by members of the staff who told them when they were 'hot' or 'cold' in their search. Completing this assignment opened the way to the thought that there is always treasure to be found in church and that every service is a treasure hunt. The treasure is greater than chocolate or candles. It is Jesus himself who is food for our souls and light for our lives. Part of the purpose of baptism is to claim this treasure for the children who are brought to us to be received into the Christian church.

We have found that there are innumerable ways in which we can lead into baptism, using a different teaching method each month. One month I took a book of names and their meanings into church. Any of the children in church could have their own names interpreted and we discovered the meanings of the names of the babies who were to be baptized. We saw the names are an important element in our personal identity and I told the congregation how painful it felt when I joined the army as a national serviceman and overnight found I had ceased to be 'Roy' and instead became 22404537 Private Lawrence. The beauty of being baptized is that I know that God, at any rate, knows me by name: to him I am 'Roy' – not 22404537. So as the baptism proper began, we saw that part of its purpose was to affirm the value of each child in the sight of God and we prayed that all the names to be given that day in baptism might be regarded as truly 'Christian' names, tokens of membership of the family of Christ.

The order of baptism that we use is a shortened and modified version of the Prayer Book service, to which we have added the presentation of a baptismal candle. After the baptism there is a vigorous final hymn, the flags and banners are returned, the congregation is blessed and dismissed, and over the coffee and squash there are endless opportunities for photographs.

We ask all our baptismal couples to come to at least one of these services before their own service is arranged. Then the staff member conducting the baptism calls at their home to show a video about the nature and purpose of baptism and to arrange the details of their own service. By the time they come to their own family baptism they will know the contents of the service and they will have signed an undertaking which roughly sums up the baptismal promises.

A few weeks after the baptism a member of our congregation will call round at the home of the baptismal family to see how they are, how they reacted to the baptism, and whether we can be of any further service to them. Details will be given of our facilities for young children – the mid-week toddler-praise services, the family services, the crèche facilities, and the parents and toddlers club. Since our usual visitor is a retired church social worker with special experience of families and children, she is also able to alert us if she feels there are any special needs of which we ought to be aware in the homes she visits. If the child who has been baptized has an older brother or sister, a Sunday School teacher will also visit the home with a personal invitation to join the Sunday School.

Once again there is no guarantee that any of this will evoke a response; but we will have shown concern, engaged in outreach, sown seeds and offered a ministry which has the potential for both evangelism and healing. The soil may sometimes seem shallow or stony, but who knows when growth may take place, particularly if we water it with continued care and prayer?

Stony or not, this soil is regularly made available to us for planting and tending. It is an opportunity we dare not ignore.

8 The Light on the Hill: Evangelism and Healing in Communities

'What makes you think that someone has heard the gospel just because you've preached it to them?' This was the question I was asked by an older Christian friend many years ago when he chanced to see me preaching in the streets of Liverpool. At first I was puzzled and then annoyed at his words because I thought he was suggesting that my preaching was inadequate or not clear enough. He went on to say that my attitude towards the people passing by was aggressive even hostile. Apparently I was shouting rather than speaking; I seemed to be angry more than caring. Even when people stopped to listen, I carried on shouting and not once did I seem to want to meet them. This was a real dent to my self-image as I imagined myself to be passionately and powerfully proclaiming the gospel in a darkened world. However, on reflection I decided my friend was right; far from hearing about a God who cared for them, those people heard aggression and disapproval. They had neither heard nor seen the good news. This was the beginning of my trying to share God's good news in better and more meaningful ways.

In fact my approach to evangelization has shifted its focus from telling people what I think they need to hear about God, to listening to them sharing their needs and hopes, their frustrations and failures. Only then can I bring into this open space of their lives that aspect of

God's love and care through the Lord Jesus Christ which will meet them at their point of need. This is how the gospel of Jesus Christ is both evangelistic and healing. It is evangelistic because the good news of Jesus is relevant to our circumstances and needs; and it is healing because God's love not only restores our relationship with him through the saving work of the Son but it also meets us at our point of need.

For the Gospel to be truly good news it must not come as an alien message but as one that speaks directly to our personal story. Consequently the Christian Church must always look for opportunities to present its message within the life of the community, rather than give the impression that in order to hear and receive its message the man or woman in the street must somehow give up their place in the community. After I was converted I joined the fellowship of an enthusiastic Protestant evangelical church; there I was told that I should leave behind my Roman Catholic world and friends in order to follow the Lord properly. As a result I alienated myself unnecessarily from my family and culture. I could never effectively share my faith as a result because it appeared to be an invitation to leave the community that had nurtured me and enter another, more private world. Of course I do not wish to undermine either the need to walk in holiness and obedience to Christ or the value of the fellowship of fellow believers. However, the intolerance of some Christians when it comes to living as part of the wider community is more reminiscent of the heavy defences round some cults than of the carpenter of Nazareth who was happy to enjoy the friendship of sinners.

Before we examine some of the possible bridges of witness into our communities we should remind ourselves of some of the advantages and difficulties of this approach to mission.

Welcome

At the heart of the gospel mission is the unshakeable belief that God actually likes us and has gone out of his way to the cross of calvary to make a saving relationship possible. I rather like the description in Mark's Gospel of the way in which Jesus chose his twelve disciples: 'Jesus went up on a mountainside and called to him *those he wanted*, and they came to him. He appointed twelve . . . *that they might be with him* and that he might send them out to preach and have authority to drive out demons' (Mark 3.13–15, my italics). Before the disciples went out they were first welcomed in, which meant entering into a relationship. We too must be prepared to build relationships which cost time and energy rather than just evangelize in order to get people into church and then out on to the streets to be a witness. It may sound like a well-worn cliché, but it still has the bite of a challenge when folk say that they have better friendship with people down at the pub than with those 'in church'. Why is this so? It is because we have lost the gift of welcome.

It is a sad affair but it seems that the Church has over the years developed as a parallel community to the wider community but somehow the two have drifted too far apart. Perhaps we need to stop and learn from our Celtic ancestors who were especially good at evangelizing their scattered communities. Professor Ian Bradley writes:

> The approach of the Celtic missionaries was essentially gentle and sensitive. They sought to live alongside the people with whom they wanted to share the good news of Christ, to understand and respect their beliefs and not to dominate or culturally condition them.[1]

I heard this story while I was conducting a conference at Scargill House in the Yorkshire Dales. Once upon a time

87

there was a young boy who was trying to open up a flower whose buds were closed. No matter how careful he tried to be he could not avoid bruising or damaging the bud as he forced it open. 'Why can't I open the flower like God does?' he asked. His mother replied, 'But dear, God opens the flower from the inside. And he only does this when the climate is right for the flower, when there is warmth and light.' The ministry of welcome is to provide that warmth and light so that people may open up their lives to God from the inside as a flower does to the sun.

Our welcome must be authentic. In other words we must be interested in the person and not just in the opportunity to win them for Jesus; if this is not going to happen then we still go on caring. Jesus cared and healed many who did not respond and become his followers. We are told that his love was still looking out for the rich young ruler even as he walked away from the challenge of becoming a follower of Jesus (Mark 10.21ff).

One way in which we show our commitment to the whole person is by living as community. There is a growing concern within the churches to recover the sense of fellowship and the shared life. Modern society has fragmented the way that people live; the commuter age has separated the place where we live from the place or places where we worship or work. More and more families 'bus' their children to school and to all the ancillary activities connected with it. We seem to have become an invisible society catching only glimpses of each other as we arrive back at the house to eat and sleep. The cities were once places where people lived but now they are often only the places where we go to work or to be entertained. Many a church has become marooned in towns where no one lives in the centre, towns with no soul because the people have moved to housing estates where they live near, but not necessarily with, other people.

The Church also has been caught in this drift; apart from services and teaching meetings there is little corporate life. But having said this the Church still retains its seeds of community in its call to be salt and light. Consequently the Holy Spirit of God will always stir us to find ways to share our lives together as a constructive group so that we may then go on to revive and resource the wider community in which we live. Our Celtic forefathers conducted their evangelism from a community base. As Michael Mitton writes:

> These monastic communities were not only places to which interested people could come and learn about the faith, but they also became schools and universities, hospitals and centres for social care of all kinds, thus drawing in large numbers of non-Christian people who encountered a community with a living faith in God.[2]

My purpose here is not to discuss the principles of community and how to recover them, but to underline the importance of finding a place of belonging in which authentic evangelism can take place. I suggest that the health of the secular community is stoked and to some degree maintained through some of the major festivals which still take place and to which most people give their support. Some have their origin within the Church and others are purely secular. It strikes me as good thing to welcome people in the love of God on occasions such as Remembrance Sunday; but it needs to be done in a way which is not intrusive yet which nonetheless offers a bridge to responding to the love of God in a healing way.

Invitation

It was Donald Coggan, the former Archbishop of Canterbury, who pointed out that the name Jesus or Joshua comes from a word which means 'to give room or space to.'[3] So much evangelism is non-productive because it seems to corner people rather than give them space into which they can step as a beginning to the journey of wholeness and healing. Henri Nouwen picks up this theme of creative and saving space when he talks about witness as hospitality and then goes on to define hospitality as space in which change can take place.[4] Witness is an offer which everyone is free to refuse, but if it is offered spaciously then there is room to return for more.

An invitation not only includes space; there has also to be clarity. In other words people must know precisely what they are being invited into in order for them to make a proper response. When I was a trainee Baptist minister in Birkenhead in the early 1970s I was asked to make a pastoral visit to a man who was due to inherit a chain of betting shops. Just before I went someone in the church told me that he was in need of salvation and that he was rather a hard man because he had 'stolen' one of the girls from the youth club. Apparently since they had been married neither she nor her husband had attended church. So I set out to visit their home and steeled myself for the moment when I would challenge him to give his life to Jesus.

When he opened his front door and realized who I was he said, 'I suppose you have been told how evil I am and have come to try and save me!' Before I could answer he went on to say, 'I would love to be a real Christian but it's too late now.' He then told me that he had left home as a young man because he did not like his father's business nor the way in which people, greedy for money, gambled away their savings and ended up in a worse situation. His travels took him to South Africa where he happened to come upon an evangelistic rally being held in a huge tent outside Johannesburg. As he was reading the noticeboard a huge hand seemed to descend from above him and grip his shoulder. He turned round to see who it was and before him stood the former heavyweight wrestling champion of South Africa who was the evangelist running the mission. 'Jesus wants you now!' barked the evangelist, who then led him inside the tent and down to the front of the meeting where he exhorted him to kneel down. The young man did so, but really because he had no idea what else he should do, he was so intimidated by this huge man. By now the evangelist was on the platform and saying, 'Friends, already one sinner has come to the foot of the cross, who will be the next?' Apparently people came forward in large numbers to join him. 'There was only one problem with the situation,' said the bookmaker. 'The decision to become a Christian was his and not mine!'

I began to understand this man and appreciate why he might have stayed away from church. I also apologized for the way he had been treated and told him that he had not been given room to think and understand what commitment was all about. He still did not understand, his rough experience had scarred him and he thought commitment to Christ was conscription rather than conversion. The simple lesson to learn was that the good news involves an invitation to live and that we must learn to befriend before we are in the privileged position to invite.

Befriending is the honest witness of telling and showing another person what being a Christian means for us. This is the time when we will be tempted to give an advert rather than a testimony. But our respect for the person we are talking to means we must tell them the truth and so share our own difficulties in the faith. Often we do not do so because we feel it would put people off; instead we present something like a glossy press cutting, rather than talking about the Jesus we love and know and combining this with our human story of the ups and downs in Christian living. Consequently friendship evangelism is a matter of trust on our part that our authentic experience of Jesus will be enough to attract someone else to follow Christ as well. Yet this costly experience of giving time and appearing vulnerable while telling the gospel story has proved to be the most effective way of bringing other people to a living faith. From John Finney's book, *Finding Faith Today*, which is a survey of how people became Christians, it appears that the majority of people who become Christians do so through the invitation and friendship of others.[5]

Challenge

At the heart of the good news is a call to live differently. By any definition this is confrontational. It is a challenge to recognize and submit willingly to the Lordship of Jesus Christ. It is disturbing and upsets the balance of life, but it cannot be avoided if true conversion is to follow. But it is also a choice. So while we cannot bludgeon people into faith, we must also be careful not to present Jesus Christ as an optional extra on the road to spirituality.

A challenge is not the same thing as a demand. While a demand leaves no room for reflection, a challenge must contain a clear sharing of facts and the opportunity to decide. One of the beautiful things about Jesus in the gospels is that people felt free enough to ask him questions. 'What must I do?' asked one. 'Are you really the Christ?' asked another. Not too long ago I was listening to the evangelist J John, speaking to ministers. He pinpointed the fact that we must allow people whom we are seeking to win to the faith to ask awkward questions like 'yes, but how?' If we are honest we do sometimes make the Christian life look easier than it actually is. There is nothing like questions to make us earth our heaven and so offer the bridge of challenge for others to walk across.

The resource of community events

The following are some suggestions of how we can build
into community events something of the loving and healing witness of the good news of Jesus. These are not hard
and fast liturgies but ideas which you might like to think
over and possibly adapt and build on for yourself.

REMEMBRANCE SUNDAY

This civic service is still a major feature of our community life almost the world over. It is attended by young
and old alike and in the United Kingdom involves the
Church of England in a central and strategic role. For
many attending it still evokes painful memories of two
world wars, while the Falklands and Gulf wars affect
younger generations. Its central feature of remembering
involves for many people painful moments which can
still hurt. Because the Church's ministry has at its heart
the Eucharist in which we hear the words of Jesus, 'Do
this in remembrance of me', I suggest that we have an
opportunity to bring the healing of Christ to memories
that may not have been yet shared with him.

I would like then to offer the following as one way of
giving people an unthreatening opportunity to remember before the Lord and receive a touch of his healing.
This is best done in the church service rather than at the
town cenotaph or war memorial. It could be introduced
by a short talk on healing of memories and then followed by this simple exercise.

Reading   John 21.15–19
Talk   The reinstatement of Peter, his opportunity to re-
          member a painful time and own it and then be
          freed from and walk in newness of life.
Exercise We all have memories. Today you may be remem-
          bering someone who has died and whose memory

you cherish. You may also be remembering a person who has died and this still leaves some hurt, some bad effect within you. Today, in the silence, I would like to give you an opportunity to bring both kinds of people and memories before God for his healing and blessing.

As you sit, let us relax and be open to God as we allow ourselves to remember.

Now using the hand you normally write with, I invite you to remember someone whose memory you find hurtful. When you know who this person is, just close your hand and silently think about this person, who they were, what they did and how this affects you.

Then simply lift up this closed hand to God and then quietly open your hand and give this person up to God, you may like to mention their name silently. Ask God to heal you and help you to get over any bad effect they may have had on your life. Now put your hand down.

Now with your other hand I invite you to think of that person who was a special friend or loved one who has made a good impression on your life. Like before, when you know who this person is, close your hand and lift them up to God. Name them and in silence just give thanks for them and all they mean to you. Then put your hand down.

Closing prayer to include request for healing of hurting memories and celebration for having had good friends.

REQUIEMS AND FUNERALS

The practicalities of funerals and the opportunity they offer for pastoral care have already been discussed in

Chapter Six. Unlike the usual parish funeral, however, a requiem is a special service of remembrance where thanksgiving is the central theme. There is a growing need in our community to offer space to people who wish to remember loved ones, especially children. This is because there is often little support for the grieving after the funeral and the expectation of their friends is that they will soon get back to normal. The sad casualty of this kind of situation is that we are given little room to appropriately cherish the person whom we have lost. This is even more so with regard to the death of children through miscarriage, still-birth and abortion. Many such parents struggle with depression afterwards because they have not been given creative space to acknowledge the true life of the child who has been lost, no matter how old the foetus. You may like to think of holding such a service for the people in your town or city who have lost a child. It would need to include the following elements:

– *The opportunity to name and acknowledge the child in question.*
This can be done by writing their name down and then having a procession to the altar with some suitably quiet music or song in progress. Then each parent can place their child's name in a basket and have a quiet moment to reflect and thank God for their life, however short. Later on the minister can lift up the basket of names and make a special offertory prayer recognizing and remembering all these lives. You may include a prayer where each parent can (simultaneously) say the name of their child aloud.
– *Something belonging to the child.*
This can be a photograph or a toy or clothes or something they have made, written or drawn. These items can be placed around the altar as a reminder that, for however long or short a time, their owners had a life and a right to life as much as anyone else.

– *A celebratory theme.*
This is not to undermine the sadness or tragedy of death, but the focus must always be on life. Something can be said about the reality of ongoing life and development in heaven with Christ and the angels.
– *The hope of the resurrection.*
While being careful not to capitalize on people's hurt feelings this is a good place to speak of Jesus's death and his return to life. You could point out that this too was a premature death but that it was not the end of the story. It is equally so for every child being remembered.
– *An opportunity to care for others.*
You could provide a collection for the work of children's hospices or some form of care for children in need.

CELEBRATING CREATION AND CREATIVITY

We live in a society where ecological and conservationist convictions are playing an increasingly important role. All too often these have become the preserve of New Age groups or a small minority of Christians who support Green Party interests. Most churches do not have a public liturgy for recognizing and celebrating their conservationist causes except perhaps for Harvest and possibly Rogation Sunday with its 'beating of the parish boundaries'. Yet celebrating creation could be an excellent opportunity to reflect the nature and the heart of our Creator God. The church could collaborate on local tidy-up or reclamation schemes and then, having shared in the hard work of transformation, ask God's blessing on the new site. There could be an annual open-air thanksgiving for green areas – a chance to thank God for giving us creative skills. The church could provide an occasion for honouring the gifts of the people in the community. How about holding a public service to give thanks for the work of all the carers in the community from doctors and nurses to counsellors and councillors?

There could be a liturgy enabling people to commit themselves to caring for others with the help of God. It could be a time for a simple laying on of hands on all such people that God would bless them for their hard work and help them to develop their skills and gifts.

CELEBRATING THE CITY

Most towns and cities contain buildings which are associated with special events both good and bad. Cathedrals are special places of worship but they also have a unique function for the community, in that more than any other building, they contain the history of that community. Consequently, to celebrate the life of a city invariably involves the life and witness of the cathedral. Cathedrals are also representative of the whole Church in the community and not just the Church of England. There are many opportunities then for the churches of a community in co-operation with the civil authorities to hold some form of celebration for the history of the town or city focused on the cathedral. This could be a festive occasion involving street parties or walks and could be held at regular intervals. It would help to strengthen community ties and demonstrate how the Church continues to play a part in making communities whole.

Communities also have scars, places where acts of evil and violence may have occurred. This is an opportunity for the Church to identify with acts of violence and evil which have taken place and offer repentance for them. There is surely a need for a walk of reconciliation in towns and housing estates which have witnessed nights of racial violence and destruction. This is not an occasion to apportion blame but to repent before the Lord for the breakdown in the life of the community. Nowadays people regularly place flowers where someone has been murdered or killed in a road accident. Such events traumatize that part of the community and there is a need for corporate healing of some description. I know, for example, that a group of church leaders went down to the railway tracks in Walton in Liverpool where the murdered body of a toddler was found. It was not announced publicly but many attended, as if acknowledging some connection with the killing by the very fact of living in that part of the city. There was in fact a shared guilt which needed to be confessed and cleansed. The little service of confession and healing helped many in that community to be set free from their shock and to get on with their lives again.

Doubtless there are many other occasions for sharing the gospel and bringing a healing moment to others. The major Christian festivals of Easter and Christmas still attract many people into church who do not normally attend. However, this chapter has sought to suggest some ideas for more public occasions and to create new liturgies of witness in the wider community. The opportunities are there and we need to be more inventive and creative about the way we share our good news. We live in a society that is fragmenting and yet people are still looking for a place to belong. The Church is under God's divine challenge to provide occasions for true community and a proper focus for belonging. These are only truly to be found in a relationship with God through his Son Jesus Christ.

9 Evangelism, Healing and Mission Strategy for All Ages

Parish mission is a day-by-day ingredient of church life. If Christians believe that the gospel can make a saving and healing difference to the hurts, follies and sins of our nation and that we are called to make this difference known and available, then mission must be worked into our ordinary church structures and programmes. We must not wait for occasional 'parish missions' to do this work for us. But having said that, I still believe there is a place for the specific parish mission project. In Prenton we aim to have a major mission event every year.

During my first year as vicar I used the fact of my own novelty as an opportunity to be the parish missioner myself during a fortnight of mission events. There were five mid-week meetings for what we called 'Eight-o'-clock Topics'. The subjects were 'What's wrong with us?', 'How does Jesus make a difference?', 'Dealing with depression', 'The conquest of fear', and 'Death is NOT the end'. Thirty people came to the first, but there were more every evening and we ended with over a hundred.

On the first Sunday there was a morning service with the topic 'Why be a Christian?' and it was followed by a family lunch. At the evening service the topic was 'What is Christian Healing?'. On the second Sunday there was a family service in the morning complete with stories, quiz questions and prizes. The evening service included an 'Any Questions?' session. By a lucky chance the fortnight ended with two televised services from St Stephen's on the last Sunday which subsequently went out nationwide. So the mission gathered momentum day by day.

The TV services were entitled 'Christian Healing Rediscovered' and 'Invitation to Healing' and they stimulated interest near and far. We had invited various people to tell their own stories of healing to BBC interviewer David Davies. They proved to be very impressive even when he put them under pressure. A young wife who had once been in a wheelchair with multiple sclerosis but now showed no sign of the disease after receiving the ministry of Christian healing, obligingly stood up and gave the viewers a twirl when asked to do so. When she was asked how she would feel about Jesus if her MS were to return tomorrow, she said that though her physical healing had been a wonderful thing, if she were told that she could only hold on to her healing by renouncing Christ she would rather go back to her wheelchair than be without Jesus, because he was the real wholeness she had found.

After the services were televised 600 people wrote or phoned to say how much they had benefited from the programmes. Some had received physical healing as they watched, but no less wonderful were the two letters from 'Bill' and 'Ben', the two atheists mentioned in Chapter Two, who wrote to say that they had rediscovered faith as they watched the programme. In this mission as in all our missionary strategy we have found it natural for evangelism and healing to go hand in hand.

Our subsequent outreach policy has often been not unlike the 'jujitsu principle' mentioned in Chapter Six. If we can save ourselves work by taking advantage of a national project rather than inventing a local one we have always done so. So it has been our policy to take a full part in any nationwide mission, such as the ones which Dr Billy Graham has conducted in Britain from time to time, or the more recent 'Minus to Plus Mission' of Reinhard Bonnke. 'Let nothing be wasted' (John 6.12) is a good motto for all forms of evangelism. However we have still found it necessary to supplement these from time to time with projects of our own.

At one stage we asked our Rural Dean to conduct an 'internal mission' for us. He met our leaders both to listen to them and encourage them in their work. He spoke to our congregations both at Parish Communion and at a healing service. He led us in a mid-week Bible study which examined the role of a local church. We appointed 'parish detectives' to find out what happens in the various organizations and activities which characterize our life together and to report back to the congregation as a whole, with a comment from the Rural Dean. The Bishop of Chester spent an evening with us confirming our Confirmation candidates and talking to us about 'Being the People of God'. We had a youth night and a family day including a bring-and-share meal and an all-age social. The basic questions for the week included: 'Is Jesus meeting our needs through our church?', 'Is Jesus meeting the needs of our parish through us?', 'How well do we know the gospel and live the gospel and share the gospel?', 'What is God saying to us now?', 'What is he calling us to be and to do?' and 'Where do we go from here?'

One of the answers that came to us was that we should plan a fortnight of mission to the neighbourhood as a whole and that it should be led by an outside missioner because by now I was the 'old vicar' rather than the new vicar and the 'It's only him' syndrome had well and truly set in as far as anything I might say in Prenton was concerned.

We therefore arranged for our diocesan missioner to spend a fortnight with us and we gave ourselves eighteen months to plan and structure it.

We set out a number of principles which would have to undergird the whole operation if it were to embody healing and evangelism. They are principles which are just as applicable to parish life as a whole as to a specific mission project.

- We must identify known groups and known needs within the community.
- We must ask whether Christ meets these needs at present through us and what else he is calling us to do.
- We must consider the idiom in which we can best communicate with each group.
- We must arrange widespread consultation within our local church so that the whole membership may contribute its knowledge and its wisdom in our enquiries.
- We must train the whole church for mission. The total membership would be more important than the missioner, though he would have a central place in pre-mission training activities as well as the mission itself.
- We must identify the talents we have within the congregation and make sure they are not wasted in our plans for outreach.
- We must cover the preparation with prayer, arranging all styles and kinds of prayer occasions so that each may worship in the style which is most natural.
- We must remember that the means of preparation should anticipate the desired result. In contrast to the worldly motto that 'the end justifies the means', for us the means should embody the end.
- We must plan not just for clear communication of the gospel but also for sufficient emotional space to ensure that there will be no improper manipulation of anyone attending a mission event.
- We must make sure there is sufficient finance available for publicity, and hospitality and all other expenses.

We spent many hours in internal seminars, think-tanks and working groups as we planned our programme and our publicity. We decided we would entitle the mission 'Opening Time'. The aim would be to open the church to the people of the parish and to open the people of the parish to the healing truth of the gospel. Our motto was 'Christ is the key'. We had some little key fobs made with the mission logo on them, so that every time we used our keys we prayed for the mission.

In order to open the church to the parish we arranged dozens of occasions of hospitality. Our missioner was licensed by the Archdeacon at a Harvest Supper, which was attended by as many of the congregation as we could fit in. There was a men's evening at a local club. A women's luncheon was arranged in the church hall, complete with wine. There were musical evenings in different idioms to appeal to different groups. The Salvation Army Band and Songsters provided one of the concerts and a Christian folk singer was 'in concert' at the other. Young parents were invited to a Brains Trust at which the missioner was joined by a child psychiatrist, a GP and a teacher to answer questions and give advice on creating a Christian home. There were 'Teddy Bears' Picnics' for the toddlers, outreach to teenagers, and a family day ending in a barn dance with a good band. Other events included house meetings which dealt with sectional interests such as local history, photography, art and gardening, with each meeting offering hospitality designed to be suitable for its distinctive clientele. It was generous hospitality and was talked about for many months afterwards. The aim was for church members to buy the heavily subsidized tickets and to bring their friends and neighbours. The tickets all bore the words, 'This event will contain a presentation of the basic truth about Jesus', so that nobody would be misinformed about the fundamental purpose of the whole programme.

Everyone who attended any of these events subsequently received a letter thanking them for coming and inviting them to a 'Christian Basics' service. I also outlined the achievements of the project in a letter in the parish magazine, as an encouragement to the congregation.

It will be apparent from all this that I do not share the view of those who say that parish missions are now outdated. I believe that there should be many more parish missions nationwide. However in all honesty I feel I should enter a caveat here. A church is nearly always better and stronger for holding a mission. Its influence can often be observed well beyond the local boundary. However in my experience missions do *not* result in an immediate influx of large numbers of outsiders into the local church. We have several steady churchgoers who joined us because they were touched by one or other of our missions, but their number is so small that I can count them on my fingers. By contrast over the years scores of people have come into the church because the day-by-day programme of church activities and the day-by-day structure of church life aims at a steady ministry of evangelism and healing.

In earlier chapters we have already looked at the needs of various groups within society and the role of the local church in meeting them. For instance the needs of the bereaved which we considered in Chapter Six can hardly be overestimated. According to a recent survey only 3 per cent of widows and widowers are visited by a caring organization after their bereavement. In our parish ministry in Prenton we have raised this figure to close to 100 per cent and there are plans to appoint a full-time worker in Wirral whose work will be to encourage all the churches in this area to launch similar bereavement support schemes. The need is so great and it is easy to be intimidated by the extent of it; but I believe that with thought and care many churches may find to their own surprise that they do have the resources to meet it. If not it may be possible to import some help. There are people nationwide who have been trained in the skills of 'Christian listening' by the Acorn Christian Healing Trust, and many of them are not being fully used. A telephone call might provide the name of someone who could supplement or even supervise a bereavement visiting team.[1]

In Chapter Seven we thought about the needs of couples who are preparing to marry. I dread the periodic solicitor's letters which arrive on our door mat requesting a copy of a marriage certificate because I know that it usually means a marriage is in serious trouble. The national statistics of separation and divorce indicate an area of pain that we cannot ignore. They remind me of the soldier who shouted out to the sergeant who was marching his squad towards a cliff, 'For God's sake say something, even if it's only goodbye!' The Church should have something to say in this situation, and it ought to be more than 'goodbye!' The Prenton scheme is not meant for a moment to be a blueprint for other churches to follow because different neighbourhoods have different social structures and different congregational resources, but I hope it may prove a stimulus to thought and prayer and action.

If we are serious about meeting physical, mental and spiritual needs in the name of Christ, there are other groups we should also consider. Here are two of them.

In my parish, as in the whole of Merseyside, I am always coming across groups of young people on the roads. Sometimes they are chatting in a desultory fashion. Sometimes they are smoking or sniffing substances of a dubious nature. Sometimes they look as though they are up to no good. Often they look as though they have not a clue what to do, where to go, what to be. How can we meet them at their point of need? A small number of them come to church, where I hope they feel a significant part of the Christian family. We try to provide interesting activities and learning opportunities. We also give them teaching opportunities! Periodically a service is handed over to our youth worship team. In one service they presented 'Christian Aid' themes to the rest of us with the help of music and dance and comedy sketches. They reminded us of the size of the world by blessing us in many languages, including sign language, and they were an object lesson in enthusiasm. But of course the majority of the young people of Prenton have no intention of darkening the door of any church. Generally it is not that they have anything against us – though you would not know it by the way in which some of them regularly break the windows of St Alban's – but for the most part they think of us as irrelevant to the world in which they live.

So we have had to enter their world. In partnership with the Local Authority we run a youth centre. Along with sports and social activities we offer thoughtful comments on employment and unemployment, the drug scene, sexuality, the neighbourhood and its problems. We teach cooking and basic first aid. If there is an obvious hurt we try to heal it. One example was the pain at every level of society after the Hillsborough disaster. We instituted a yearly football match between Prenton Youth Club and the Hillsborough Boys Club with a silver cup which commemorates a local victim of the disaster. One year Prenton goes to Hillsborough and the next year Hillsborough comes to Prenton.

None of this may sound particularly religious, and maybe we err on the side of caution in seeking to share our faith, but recently we had a reminder that both the young people and the other members of the community who use the centre do know something of our motivation in providing it. The Local Authority was facing severe financial problems and reacted by a variety of economy measures including cutting our grant. Suddenly the youth centre was facing bankruptcy and by the terms of the trust deed I was forced to announce that the centre would close within a few weeks. I was amazed to find that the community suddenly shed its accustomed apathy. Thirty members of the community met and we found ourselves praying together. The young people launched a series of fund-raising activities, a committee of 'friends' was formed with its own fund-raising programme. Inspired by this, I set aside a fortnight to approach businesses and charities for help. Scores of letters were written, supplemented by telephone calls and visits. We needed £20,000 to save the centre. Amazingly within a few weeks we had it.

There was a feeling in the community that the whole rescue operation had been mysteriously blessed, that there was a power at work among us we did not altogether understand. It was at this point that the users of the centre asked for a service of thanksgiving. They also asked that a large cross should be put on the wall of the main hall in the centre. I wonder whether it is fanciful to say that this was an unarticulated recognition that Jesus had met us at our point of need.

Another group with many needs is the elderly, particularly the housebound elderly. Like most churches we try to minister to the spiritual needs of this group by giving out hundreds of home communions every year. We also run a monthly luncheon club, and since for elderly and lonely people the worst day of the year is Christmas Day, for years we have provided a full Christmas Day dinner in the church hall followed by entertainment and carol-singing. One year one of our guests wrote to me to say that quite literally the Christmas dinner had saved her life, stopping her from committing suicide. Over the years this has increasingly been an ecumenical activity, and now it has moved to a

Methodist church where the new kitchen facilities are better.

It would not be difficult to extend the list of people around us who are there to be met at their point of need in the name of Christ if we are willing and available: people who are sick, stressed, busy or bored, housewives whose tiny children are driving them to distraction, a growing number of mentally sick people who are supposed to be receiving 'community care', and professional carers who may feel that nobody actually cares about them!

I believe it is for each local church to know its local situation, people and needs, and to plan a focused pastoral programme. We are so often *un*focused: a little visit here, a little visit there, a chat with Mrs Brown, a cup of tea with Mrs Green. I do not undervalue any of it, but the church is called to healing and evangelism, to spiritual warfare, to a campaign for the kingdom. A vague and casual ministry will not suffice. We need to be focused in our aims, strategies and activities.

Moreover our focus must not blur when we reach the edge of our own locality. I am writing this chapter at a time of appalling catastrophe in Rwanda. Thousands of people, many of them small children, are dying week by week. It is a self-inflicted wound, but it would be no help to tell that to the children or to any of the other victims who just happen to be in the wrong place at the wrong time.

What does it mean to be a healing church at a time like this? Unicef has made an appeal to the churches for prayers and a collection, and so we said our prayers and put a collection box at the back of our churches. At the end of the day there was over £200 in the boxes. That completed our involvement – or so I thought. But I reckoned without God and without a member of our congregation called Hilda. Hilda came to me at the back of the church and I told her, perhaps a little smugly, that we had over £200 in the box. 'It won't do', she said very quietly but firmly. 'I believe that God has told me we must send £1,000 and send it now. If you will ask the treasurer to send £1,000 now I will guarantee that the other £800 will come from somewhere.' The church-wardens and I hovered about her rather uncertainly. We do give a tenth of our income away in any case, but £800 would make a hole in this amount and we did not want to reduce the sum we had planned to send to other good causes. 'How about £500, Hilda?' I asked tentatively. Gently she answered, 'When God says £1,000, we can't offer him less.' Another church member said 'Perhaps £600?' '£1,000', said Hilda. I obtained the cheque for £1,000 and took it to Hilda. 'Are you sure about this?' I asked. 'I'll post it', she answered, and so she did.

Before next Sunday people had come from all over the parish to Hilda's front door with cheques and bank notes. Within a week we had £1,000 and soon we were well on our way to a second £1,000!

Inside and outside our parish it is our job, our *raison d'être*, to be the hands, the feet, the heart and the wallet of the healing Christ. It would be very sad to settle for a lesser concept of the church. I am aware, though, that Christian healing and Christian evangelism can be made to sound too easy. In one sense it is right that they should sound easy because God provides the resources for both. Our own best ideas and efforts will be useless unless they are channels for his power. However as Dr Stanley Thomas has said, 'Healing is costly work, demanding not only preparation, time, skill and labour, but oneself. For the Christian Healer, as for the healing Christ, there is a cross at the heart of it.'[2] The same can be said about evangelism.

To evangelize and heal in the name of Christ is to do battle with half-understood forces. It is not only to do battle but mysteriously it is to become the battlefield oneself. Moreover the battle does not become easier with the passage of years.

So there has to be a pain warning. Jesus was not speaking idly when he talked of discipleship in terms of 'taking up our cross'.

The Church is called to think at least three times – first, about the great commission set before us to 'preach and heal', second, about the great resources offered to us in God the Father, God the Son, and God the Holy Spirit, and then third, aout the cost of discipleship. If, having thought about these things, we decide to trust and obey – a certain amount of hell may break out; but then the healing power of heaven may also break in!

10 Evangelism and Healing: Great Expectations?

In the early 1970s I was leading an evangelistic mission on a council estate in Birkenhead. Over 600 people had come forward at the gospel invitation to make a commitment of faith and to receive some basic counselling to help them follow up their decision to become a Christian. Of the 600 who had signed decision cards, fewer than thirty were seriously interested when they were later visited in their homes. Needless to say, I was shocked and upset that there was so little true conversion and spent the next few weeks examining where we had failed. The team had worked hard and very well together; there had been plenty of prayer and the counselling offered was of good quality. This particular mission also included an opportunity to receive prayers for healing and again hundreds had responded; but to my knowledge only one or two people seemed to receive any healing benefit from it. So where had we gone wrong?

The answer lay between the twin peaks of expectation and experience. Our faith needs to be aware of the reality of a situation as well as challenging it to be changed by the power and promises of God. On the one hand we need to avoid empty triumphalism and on the other we must be careful not to dampen faith in the power and workings of God. We have to keep a balance between realism and vision. This chapter looks at our expectations and then offers some reflections based on experience.

Expectations for mission

THE GOD WHO ACTS

Bishop Michael Marshall has written that what we need today is 'a theology of the God event' in order to recapture a sense of expectation for effective mission.[1] He rightly places the focus for evangelism and healing within the initiative of God. Neither of these enterprises is the result of emotionalism or manipulation. They originate from within the heart of our God who cares for his whole creation and who has taken steps to bring humankind into a saving knowledge of himself.

One of the ways in which God demonstrates his willingness to act is by offering a promise. There are over 200 references to promises in the Bible and they range from God's promise to Abraham that he would become a father of nations, to the promise of eternal life to those who believe in Jesus Christ. God's promises build up our trust in him, inspiring us to act in anticipation that he will also act. Consequently when Jesus's followers accepted his commission to go out and make disciples of all nations, they expected God to act too, and so their witness flooded throughout the four known corners of civilization.

In the realm of the healing ministry there is the example of Peter and John acting out the activity of Jesus when they pray for the lame man outside the temple at the gate beautiful. Peter knows that the initiative and the power to act for healing does not belong to him. 'Silver and gold I do not have', he says, 'but what I have I give you. In the name of Jesus Christ of Nazareth, walk' (Acts 3.6). Peter is in fact responding to the word of the Lord and translating it into action and expectation on behalf of the lame man. Although the text itself does not say so, it implies that Peter senses the divine moment in which it is appropriate to act. This is also demonstrated by the words of Mary when she accepts the divine initiative and purpose for her life, to be the mother of Christ. She says to the angel, 'May it be to me as you have said' (Luke 1.38).

Whenever we respond to the promising word of God we shall be changed and see changes. This is the testimony of Scripture. To quote Michael Marshall again, 'We need to stir up again a new sense of expectation in a God who acts, not by capricious intervention . . . but according to his promises and according to a plan in which each of us has a place and a purpose.'[2]

PEOPLE WHO ARE PREPARED

All four Gospels witness to the fact that part of the build-up to the activity of God in mission is Jesus's exhortation to the disciples to prepare for what is to come. The time they spent in the upper room after the crucifixion may well have been for some a way of avoiding public contact with the Jews because they were afraid of being arrested, but for God it was time preparing for the coming of the Holy Spirit in power. Consequently, on the eve of his ascension into heaven, Jesus commanded his disciples to wait in the city until they were clothed with God's power (Luke 24.49). It is this power through the Holy Spirit which would enable them to witness to Jesus Christ in what they say and do (Acts 1.8).

One priceless lesson to take from this episode is that true evangelism is not a rush into the arena of the needy; people in need will always be there demanding our attention. Rather it is a waiting on God for empowerment, direction and timing. It was this correct use of time which enabled the disciples to recognize the right time to co-operate with God in his saving purposes. The correct use of time prepared them to receive the power of the Holy Spirit to engage in mission. When the Spirit came upon them their response was first to worship and then to witness. It is essential that this is the order of events. Otherwise our mission can become a mere sharing of dogma or can degenerate into an aggressive diatribe of telling others that they are lost but we are saved.

When the Holy Spirit guides our work of mission, he enables us to share the word not in opposition to where others stand but alongside them. This is after all the cutting edge of mission, that the word of God comes to where people are, not where they should be. One reason why Jesus was in constant conflict with the religious authorities was that he seemed to be too friendly with sinners for their liking, because he was concerned to get alongside them. Peter's sermon on the day of Pentecost addressed the issues of the Messiah, eternal life and survival and of how David was a type and forerunner of the true king of Israel, the very issues that brought the majority of pilgrims into Jerusalem. For those pilgrims the word of God through Peter spoke to their condition and need at the most appropriate time.

There is of course another issue which waiting will draw into clearer perspective and that is the credulity gap we often carry within our hearts. Do we actually expect anything to happen when we pray for healing or go and share the good news? If not, we need to acknowledge our doubts before God, and seek to deepen our relationship with Jesus Christ. All the attempts made by the disciples to heal and witness, whether successful or abortive, stem from their having spent time in close relationship with Jesus. The outpouring of the Holy Spirit at Pentecost was a high point in this developing relationship; now that they were filled with the Spirit, the disciples knew that Christ lived ever more deeply in their lives. The action of mission then does not come out of our enthusiastic or panicked sense that we ought to be doing it; it rather results from being still and waiting for

God's time. Then we may be fully confident that he will act. 'For the word of power issues out in silence; the word of motivation issues out of stillness; and the word of change issues straight out of stability that requires that special staying power, in season and out of season.'3

WITNESS AND TESTIMONY

We all need encouragement if we are to continue to focus on God's power to act. One way to do this is through pilgrimage, whether we journey to the healing shrine of Lourdes in Southern France or the airport Vineyard church in Toronto where many people report extraordinary blessings of refreshing and renewal. Pilgrimage meets our need to be in places and among people where God has acted powerfully and brings us back into contact with the God who acts. This is also why a knowledge of the saints is so important; to some degree they are the people who, through their piety and faith, encountered the wonderful workings of God. Through being in the places where they once lived or going to the shrines where their mortal remains lay, we make a parallel journey of faith with them, revealing our longing to be touched by the God of power with whom they were so familiar.

There is also the value of witness and testimony, which are to be found both in Scripture and in the stories of Christian friends. The Bible contains many accounts of God's dealings with his people, while our stories contain our personal experience of God in action. Stories are a powerful medium by which we are led to identify with the person concerned and perceive ways in which we too may be part of the ways in which God acts. Story is a sacrament of exhortation. It helps to bring pictures of faith to people's hearts rather than just principles of theological awareness. Pictures act like bridges which we are invited to cross to enter the places and spaces where

God is liable to act. Consequently we must endeavour to tell our story accurately and without exaggeration or distortion.

This is why Dr Peter May, a member of the Christian Medical Fellowship, has questioned so many claims of miracles among Christians. He wonders whether the stories told convey all the factors concerned in a person's healing; if they do not we have an inaccurate picture of what God may be doing when healing is requested. Our stories are gifts from God, not so that other people may duplicate our experience, but that they may be encouraged to expect God to act powerfully among us. This is especially so in the realm of healing. We must not tip the scales of story and imply that my experience of healing means that you can have an identical one. We have been called by God to pray for healing, but until God gives a true prophetic word we have not been called to promise it to certain people.

At one time when I was an incumbent of two parishes in Leicestershire I found it particularly difficult to develop a healing service which I had inherited from my predecessor. I cancelled the service and started examining the factors which lay behind this intransigence. During this time a member of the congregation came to see me about a matter of deep concern to him which involved a long breakdown in relationship with his younger brother. This had consumed my friend to such a degree that he was continually restless and unable to settle down and grow as a Christian. After some counsel and prayer he found himself face to face with his brother and with God's grace confessed his bitterness and hatred and asked for forgiveness. His brother was equally moved to be open and the result was that the two brothers were reconciled after many years of division. After seeking my permission Brian (not his real name) shared his story with the Easter Sunday morning congregation and went on to ask their

116

forgiveness for being so awkward and asked them to help him and his wife to become better involved with the church. The effect was quite powerful; it resulted in a stream of people seeking reconciliation with others and eventually opened the doors to beginning a new approach to the healing ministry.

Brian's story soon got around the small town community and these healing services began to attract over 200 people. An ecumenical healing service was born which brought relief and healing to many many people. Brian's testimony had struck a chord in a lot of hearts and began a chain reaction of blessing and release among that community. His story has also been the catalyst in other churches for forgiveness and subsequent blessing and healing.

Stories of God's activities in our lives therefore are often vehicles to stimulate others to expect God to work as powerfully. I have also found that the weaker and more vulnerable the storyteller the more powerful the response amongst the listeners.

It is right and legitimate to raise expectation so that we might be more open to the God who acts. However, in order to be truly balanced in our work of mission we must also set our expectation alongside our experience.

Experience of mission

Some years ago I and another person were preparing a seminar on the subject of healing and suffering for approximately 1,000 teenagers. I asked my fellow-speaker what he intended saying on the subject of healing. He replied to the effect that he was going to tell them that Jesus in the Bible said that they would be able to go and do greater things than him (John 14.12). Consequently he was going to encourage them to go home and seek out all who were blind and command them to receive their sight; all those confined to wheelchairs would be asked to get up out of their seats and walk; and all those who were deaf would receive their hearing again. 'Just think,' he said, 'we will be commissioning an army of healers who will go through their towns and see a powerful release of the healings of God!' Now as much as I believe in the Christian healing ministry, I was deeply concerned by this rather oversimplistic and triumphalist approach to the healing ministry which failed to take into account the facts of suffering, the need for palliative care and the value of medicine and counselling care. So I told him that if he said this I would follow his talk by saying that it would not work! This was in fact what happened.

It needs to be recognized that there is often a great difference between our expectations and our experience and wise Christians have their eyes fixed on both issues. We must beware of falling into one of two dangers when our expectations are not fully realized.

The first danger is arrogance, where we maintain that God will still act with power once the sin or disobedience or lack of faith in others is overcome. This is a form of denial which is unable to face the fact that despite powerful examples of God at work, the Bible also gives instances of limited effectiveness. The call of Isaiah (Isaiah 6) and the inability of Jesus to work miracles because of the townspeople's unbelief are evidence of this (Mark 6.5).

The other danger is cynicism and despair which can lead us to abandon mission and our faith. These are the moments when we are hurt and vulnerable and are in danger of concluding that God has let us down or that his promises are false. It is quite similar to the mood of those on the Emmaus road who when asked by Jesus what troubled them so much replied by saying, 'we had hoped' (Luke 24.21). This abandoned hope had driven them away from the city in which rumours were circulating that Jesus was alive and prevented them from recognizing him. Abandoned hopes blind us to the presence of God and the works of his power. So Jesus first listens to their complaint and then, by explaining the Scriptures to them, tells them the rest of the story which their disappointments had blinded them to seeing. C. S. Lewis once said that cynicism was the occupational hazard of every serious thinking Christian. When our experiences do not match up to our expectations we can easily become bitter and even hostile to the testimony of others when they share their experiences of God's powerful acts. Cynicism and arrogance need to be confessed for the sins that they are so that we can regain the balance of appropriate hope and belief.

The following are three areas where expectation and experience conflict. They are in fact modelled on the life and experience of Jesus.

THERE WILL BE MORE PAIN

The expectation that pain will disappear and disappointment when it does not is especially characteristic of the Christian healing ministry, precisely because we have experienced some level of healing. It is the believer who suffers more than the unbeliever because the latter, in the face of a lack of healing, may well be disappointed but not surprised. The believer is more than disappointed because he or she has experienced some healing and is left with the often unanswered question of 'why?' Jesus on the cross also screams out the question why but is not answered either. This tells me that it is OK to ask the question even if there is no answer. The temptation is to try and find an answer and all too easily fall into the trap of blaming the unhealed person, thereby causing them further suffering.

This is where the pain of caring and mission originates and if we are not careful we can become stuck with our recriminations and accusations and doubts. By sharing his scream, Jesus surrendered to God what could not be answered and then moved on in his experience of the cross. I remember attending a funeral at which it was not the minister of the church but the widower who gave the address. He began by crying out to God, asking why his wife had to die in such a painful way and take so long to die (she was the victim of a car crash and had been crushed to death). He said that he had asked God why so many times but had received no answer, he did not know why his wife had to die like she did. Then he went on to say that he did know that Jesus had died and was buried. He knew that Jesus had risen from the dead and some day would return and reunite all believers together. Then came his conclusion which I have always found helpful: that what he *did* know helped him to live with what he did not know!

If we allow our experience to eclipse our expectation then our hope merely expresses our ability to be optimistic. If we allow our expectation to steam-roller aside our experience then we lose touch with reality and can appear callous and hard. The pain of mission is that we are called to live by the experience of the cross and in the expectation in the upper room at Pentecost at the same time. It is only pain because we have tasted the powers of God but do not see that power displayed everywhere. So if we want to be the people who will engage in the mission of the Church, then we must walk the same round as Jesus.

THERE WILL BE MORE WEAKNESS

Henri Nouwen has pointed out that often those who are effective in some form of ministry are themselves handicapped with suffering and various weaknesses. He was tackling the misconception that in order to be effective we must be successful people and free from any problems or blemishes. Nothing could be further from the truth.

The apostle Paul, when writing to the Corinthian church, went out of his way to shine the spotlight on his weaknesses more than in any other letter he wrote.

Why should this be? Perhaps because these two letters have the most to say about God's power and in particular the charismatic gifts for ministry; and one of the first things mission teaches us is that God will make us weak in order to show us that the power to heal and save belongs to him alone.

Some years ago I was approached by a grandmother and asked if I would pray for her grand-daughter who was struggling with leukemia. As preparation before visiting the family I studied the Scriptures on the subject of healing and read a couple of books by two prominent leaders in the healing ministry. I prayed my best prayer and then returned home. Shortly afterwards the grandmother telephoned me to say that sadly the little girl had died and thanked me for my concern and prayers. Naturally I was sad and somewhat disappointed but not surprised. Imagine therefore my distress when the same grandmother once more came to see me over a year later to report that the child's older sister was now also struggling with leukemia. Would I come and pray for this girl also? I said no. I asked the lady if she would go and get someone else who had more success in their healing prayers. I felt so weak and ineffective and was not sure if my prayers would really help. However, this grandmother persisted and persuaded me to go and pray. This time I did not read the biographies and teachings of the greats but could only come before God and share with him my weaknesses and limitations. While I am sure that I was not the only person to pray for the older sister and I am equally sure that she had the best medical attention, I am happy to report that she had a remission of her symptoms and is still leading a full life some ten years later.

I do not know why one sister lived and the other died. My prayers I believe were sincere on both occasions. The only difference was that the second time I was in touch with my own weakness and found that it was not a barrier to praying. Once again we must learn from Jesus, the supreme wounded healer who through the great wound of the cross was still able to pray and be a way for salvation and healing.

THERE WILL BE MORE CONFLICT

As we have pointed out elsewhere in this book, to engage in mission is to invite a clash between the kingdom of God and the kingdom of darkness. Consequently we need to take this into consideration whenever we seek to serve and take proper care, protection and account- ability for whatever we do. A good example of this is the account of the healing of the man with the withered hand on the sabbath in Luke 6. Luke tells us that the Pharisees watched Jesus closely to see if he would heal on the sabbath and if he did they would have good grounds to accuse him of breaking the law (v.7). We are also told that before he spoke the word of healing, Jesus looked round at them all (v.10). This was no blind rush- ing into ministry without regard to the consequences. Jesus took his time to weigh up the situation and its repercussions if he were to heal.

Our experience of mission is to make us wise regard- ing the conflicts we may face both with people and the powers of darkness. Sometimes, but not always by any means, the stumbling block to healing or recovery can be a hold on a person or a community by a demonic power. Jesus had discernment and knew when to pray the prayer of healing and when to give the command for deliverance. Consider the young man in Mark 9 who seemed to have some form of epilepsy. Jesus commanded a deaf and dumb spirit to leave him and so the boy recovered. There is no record of Jesus praying for heal- ing for it was not an illness the boy had but some form of possessive state which once removed allowed health to return naturally. This is not to suggest, however, that sickness, whether mental or physical, is automatically to be attributed to the forces of evil. Such cases are very rare indeed.

There has been a movement over the last few years towards considering the role of unhealed community memory in acting as a barrier to hearing and receiving the good news. C. Peter Wagner and Edward Silvoso are two of the main protaganists in this field of enquiry. They recommend a healthy survey of the history of community life and some understanding of the wounds of history which may need addressing before the word of God can be properly proclaimed and received. This to some degree is an enquiry into corporate memory and its effect on the individuals and groups which make up our communities.

No so long ago I was preaching in the Republic of Ireland and during the course of one of my sermons happened to refer to Oliver Cromwell. I spoke about his military campaigns in Ireland and of how he delivered the menacing threat to Catholics who would not be cleared off their lands and be coralled in the west of Ireland. He said that they would 'go to Hell or Connaught'. Immediately I felt the temperature in the room drop considerably and I realized that there had been a deep response to the mention of this name. I paused in my sermon and mentioned this fact. Someone immediately replied that they still had not forgotten what Cromwell had done and that this person was still disposed to mistrust all Protestants. He concluded by saying, 'I won't forgive him for what he did to me and my family!' I learnt that the Irish people had long memories and that they nurtured such things until they had redress or healing. I am not exaggerating the sense of power of memory I felt in that room: it is an experience I will never forget. It also led me to think about the way such corporate events linger in the mind of the group long after they have happened and act as a barrier to listening to others. Part of the response we need to make in times of conflict is to understand the history and the development of such barriers to hearing and with the grace of God learn to listen to it and build bridges of communication; then we may have earned the right and the power to speak.

When I was an incumbent in Leicester and suggested to the PCC the possibility of a mission a few years ahead I was immediately faced with a storm of disagreement as one after the other told me of the fears such an event would cause. This was a conflict of misunderstanding and set me on a course to listen and teach about what mission really is. The experience taught me not to conclude that God is impotent but to ask the question: what is the lesson I need to hear from this?

In conclusion I would like to list a few pointers which may help us to reach more of our expectations and learn from our experiences at the same time.

1. We need to have a mature understanding of what Christian healing actually is. It is much more than merely curing people. It includes being there alongside people and in touch with their need even if they do not recover. Healing involves listening and forgiving and helping someone to come to a good end when they die.

2. We must know the people we are seeking to communicate good news to. This entails understanding their language and culture. If we fail to do this then we do not know their needs to which we wish to bring the relevant word of God.

3. Research has shown that more peole are brought to mission meetings through their friendship with Christians than by the powerful draw of the individual preacher. We must learn from the example of

Andrew who introduced his brother Peter to Jesus. Friendship takes time and commitment but it is effective. So perhaps we should set our sights on the attainable rather than dream of being someone greater.

4. We must learn the difference between praying for healing and promising healing. We are commanded to do the first but we have no mandate for the second unless God makes this very clear through some gift of revelation. Otherwise we falsely raise other people's hopes and make God a liar.

5. Expectation is a conviction of the Holy Spirit and not the product of our wanting. It is the gift which comes with the anointing of the Holy Spirit, and is never produced by our enthusiasm.

Expectation and experience are not mutually exclusive but two necessary allies. I think it is true to say that our experiences will never match our expectations. This is not to say that God cannot do more than we think for after all he is the God of surprises (Ephesians 3.20). It is more a reference to the fact that we are limited, fallen and wounded people who nevertheless have been called by God to do great things in his name. We make mistakes, we do not always hear clearly what God is saying. But failing in no way makes the expectation invalid because without it we would have no guide or target to aim for. Experience is a learning curve which helps us to reflect on the reasons for our expectations. We need not limit our expectations but we must learn the difference between what we want and what God is actually saying and equipping us to do at the moment. That is why the maxim of William Carey, the former cobbler from Northampton and founder of the Baptist Missions still holds good for us today: 'Expect great things from God, attempt great things for God.'

APPENDIX A: Check-list for the Ministry of Christian Healing

1. Can you answer the question 'What is the ministry of Christian healing?'
2. Has your church studied the biblical background to this ministry?
3. Do you understand the authority for it?
4. Do you understand the resources for it?
5. Do you understand the channels for it?
6. How many of these channels are embodied in the life of your church?
7. Can you identify an actual instance of Christian healing in the life and ministry of your church?
8. If your answer is 'yes', what is God saying to you as a consequence of this?
9. If your answer is 'no', what is God saying to you as a consequence of this?
10. Does your church hold regular services of Christian healing?
11. Has your church held a school of healing paryer?
12. Do you have regular prayer groups which undertake a ministry of healing?
13. Do you have chains of prayer to minister to immediate needs for healing?
14. Has your Church Council identified the main areas of need in your locality?
15. Have you discussed how Jesus can meet people at these points of need through your church?
16. Do you see Christian giving in terms of a healed attitude to money?

17. Is pastoral visiting linked to the healing ministry in your church?
18. Do you offer the laying on of hands with prayer when visiting the sick?
19. Do you offer the ministry of anointing when appropriate?
20. Do you offer the ministry of deliverance when appropriate?
21. Does your church have a system of bereavement care and support which involves the laity as well as the clergy?
22. Have you a system of wedding preparation which involves laity as well as clergy?
23. What provision does your church make for aftercare if marriages go wrong?
24. Have you a system of baptismal preparation and follow-up which involves laity as well as clergy?
25. What provision does your church make for counselling those who have problems, or listening to those who need to talk?
26. Have your church leaders discussed your healing ministry with medical members of your congregation?
27. Have you explored the resources available through the Acorn Christian Healing Trust?
28. How many of your church's weekday activities are relevant to the Christian healing ministry?
29. Are there any activities in the life of your church which are totally irrelevant to the healing work of Christ, or even contraproductive in terms of Christian healing?
30. If so, should they be discontinued?
31. Is your concern for Christian healing confined to your own locality and the people in it, or does it extend to the hurts of the world as a whole?
32. If so, how is this reflected in the financial policies and practices of your church and its members?

33. How is it reflected in the structure of your church services, and in the context of prayer meetings and in your other activities?
34. What else is Jesus calling you and your church to do and be, so that his healing power may come into your neighbourhood and into the wider world through you?

APPENDIX B: Check-list for the Ministry of Evangelism

1. Can you answer the question 'What is the task of evangelism?'
2. Why should your church evangelize?
3. What would you say are the main principles for engaging in mission?
4. What would you say is the basic process of sharing the good news?
5. What is the single most important thing you wish to say to others as you evangelize?
6. Is this being communicated clearly and in a style that is acceptable and effective?
7. Will you be training a team or the church to take part in mission?
8. If your answer is 'yes', have you identified the talents and gifts of your congregation or fellowship?
9. What major ingredients will you put into the training and preparation of your church?
10. Has your church identified the main needs in your locality?
11. If your answer is 'yes', have you decided on the best way to present the good news to those particular needs?
12. Make sure that you have a way of mission that your church can live with as opposed to one that it cannot live with.
13. Have you thought about having a mission audit as part of your preparation for evangelization?
14. If your answer is 'yes', does your audit include:

    – the various age-groups in your constituency;
    – the employment/unemployment figures;

      – some idea of the housing conditions;

      – the important social/public events in your area;

      – a short history of your area including reference to recurring social and spiritual problems;

      – a timetable of preparation up to the beginning of your mission;

      – how you envisage continuing the work of evangelism?

      – do you have a programme for how you will integrate new Christians into your existing fellowship?

      – an asessment of whether you are ready and able to engage in evangelism.

15. How does your church listen to the needs of people before proclaiming the word of God?

16. What provision does your church make for counselling those who share the problems which people reveal at a time of mission?

17. How would your church handle the need for deliverance?

18. Have you consulted and offered to work with the other churches in your area when planning a mission?

19. What would you do when a person from another church background makes a profession of faith at one of your meetings?

20. How would you model or include the ministry of Christian healing in your work of mission?

21. Have you considered the various costs of evangelism and mission?

      – the amount of time given to preparation and action;

      – how much money have you budgeted for mission from your overall financial resources?

      – the emotional demands of sustaining the momentum and interest in continuing mission;

also the demands of other people's expectations
of us;
- the stresses of managing differing opinions,
styles, failures, personalities and sexes;
- spiritual warfare which is often indicated in the
strain on personal health, friction in relationships and rejection and opposition from within
church and community to the idea and practice
of mission.

22. What do you think will be the main feelings and
concerns once a particular mission is over?
23. What else is Jesus calling you and your church to do
and be, so that his good news for the whole person
may be known in your neighbourhood and in the
wider world through you?

Notes

Chapter One

1 Quoted in Michael Marshall, *The Gospel Connection* (Darton, Longman & Todd 1991), p. 36.
2 Lawrence Crabb, *Finding God* (Scripture Press 1994), p. 17.
3 *Finding God*, p. 173.
4 Quoted in E. Stanley Jones, *The Christ of Every Road* (Hodder & Stoughton 1935), p. 35.
5 Eugene H. Peterson, *The New Testament in Contemporary English* (NavPress 1993).
6 Thomas Cahill, *How the Irish Healed Civilization* (Hodder & Stoughton 1995).
7 William Barclay, *New Testament Words* (SCM Press 1964), p. 104.
8 *New Testament Words*, p. 104.

Chapter Two

1 These words of Morris Maddocks originated in a broadcast interview. Subsequently they have become a sort of motto for the Acorn Christian Healing Trust.

Chapter Three

1 John Wilkinson, *Health and Healing* (Handsel Press 1980), p. 11.
2 Morris Maddocks, *The Christian Healing Ministry* (SPCK 1985), p. 49.

Chapter Five

1 C. S. Lewis, *The Screwtape Letters* (Geoffrey Bles, The Centenary Press 1942), p. 9

2 Jim McManus, *Healing in the Spirit* (Darton, Longman & Todd 1994), p. 106.

3 Jeffrey Burton Russell, *The Devil: Perceptions of Evil from Antiquity to Primitive Christianity* (Cornell University Press 1987), pp. 221–2.

4 J. B. Phillips, *The New Testament in Modern English* (Geoffrey Bles 1965), pp. 335–6.

5 Ray Steadman, *Spiritual Warfare* (Multnomah 1975), p. 48.

6 Tom White, *Breaking Strongholds* (Servant Publications 1993), p. 24.

Chapter Eight

1 Ian Bradley, *The Celtic Way* (Darton, Longman & Todd 1973), pp. 74ff.

2 Michael Mitton, *Restoring the Woven Cord* (Darton, Longman & Todd 1995), p. 94.

3 Donald Coggan, *Convictions* (Hodder & Stoughton 1975), p. 272.

4 Henri Nouwen, *Reaching Out* (Collins 1976), p. 69.

5 John Finney, *Finding Faith Today* (Bible Society 1992), p. 41.

Chapter Nine

1 Contact the Acorn Headquarters, Whitehill Chase, High Street, Bordon, Hants (tel. 01420 478121).

2 Stanley Thomas, *Journey into Wholeness* (Moorleys Print and Publishing).

Chapter Ten

1 *The Gospel Connection*, pp. 60–1.
2 *The Gospel Connection*, pp. 61–2.
3 *The Gospel Connection*, p. 61.
4 For a fuller treatment of failure see Russ Parker, *Free to Fail* (Triangle 1992).

Also available from

TRIANGLE

Books by Russ Parker

FREE TO FAIL

Everyone fails – including Christians who have been touched by the healing power of God. This compelling book explores the problems that many people have in facing up to failure and accepting its place in their Christian life.

HEALING DREAMS
Their power and purpose in your spiritual life

Why do you dream? What effect do dreams have on your waking life? How can you interpret their meaning? This expanded edition of an SPCK bestseller includes a new chapter on working and praying with dreams, showing how they can lead you closer to God and to a deeper awareness of his will.

TRIANGLE

Books
can be obtained from all good bookshops.
In case of difficulty, or for a complete list of our books,
contact:
SPCK Mail Order
36 Steep Hill
Lincoln
LN2 1LU
(tel: 01522 527486)